2.000x
Minuten-Training
ENGLISCH
Grammatik

Susan Lawrence

Compact Verlag

© 1998 Compact Verlag München
Redaktion: Barry Sandoval, Andrea Schaufler
Umschlaggestaltung: Inga Koch
Printed in Germany
ISBN 3-8174-7299-4
7272991

Inhalt

Vorwort

Der praktische Compact Aktiv-Test ermöglicht es Ihnen, Ihre Englischkenntnisse schnell und auf einfache Weise zu vertiefen, aufzufrischen und zu überprüfen.

Die kurzweiligen Übungen in einem handlichen Format machen den Aktiv-Test zur idealen Trainingsmöglichkeit für zwischendurch – ob in Bus oder Bahn, an der Haltestelle, im Wartezimmer, in der Mittagspause oder zu Hause.

Mit 2.000 Einzelübungen umfasst das Buch die wichtigsten Regeln und Sonderfälle der englischen Grammatik.

Schreiben Sie Ihre Lösungen einfach ins Buch! Die richtigen Lösungen sind stets auf der gegenüberliegenden Seite angegeben.

Mit dem Compact Aktiv-Test und einem Bleistift haben Sie die Grundausrüstung, um Ihre Englischkenntnisse in Minutenschnelle zu trainieren. Viel Spaß!

1. "A" OR "AN"? Tragen Sie den richtigen Artikel ein!

a. Travis has bought _ _ _ _ _ _ new suit.

b. Mary had to wait for _ _ _ _ _ _ hour in the rain.

c. Roger has _ _ _ _ _ _ unusual job.

d. When he became a police officer he had to buy _ _ _ _ _ _ uniform.

e. On the way home, Danny bought _ _ _ _ _ _ newspaper.

f. Doctors recommend that we should eat _ _ _ _ _ _ orange every day.

g. A screwdriver is _ _ _ _ _ _ useful tool.

h. My Uncle Bob is _ _ _ _ _ _ interesting man.

i. He tried to cross the Atlantic in _ _ _ _ _ _ beautiful yacht.

j. The new airport is _ _ _ _ _ _ arresting sight.

k. Cambridge is _ _ _ _ _ _ prestigious university.

l. He does things in _ _ _ _ _ _ unusual way.

m. He had _ _ _ _ _ _ hard time figuring out what Jill wanted.

n. Irving never seems to have _ _ _ _ _ _ new idea.

o. Paul has _ _ _ _ _ _ arrogant attitude.

2. THIS, THAT, THESE, THOSE Welches Wort passt in die Lücke?

a. She owns _ _ _ _ shop over there; she owns _ _ _ _ shops over there.

b. It won't be finished _ _ _ _ week, but you'll have it by Monday.

c. Would you rather take _ _ _ _ place next to me or _ _ _ _ one:
   would you and your husband rather take _ _ _ _ places next to me or _ _ _ _?

d. "Forget it!" he shouted, and with _ _ _ _ words he left.

e. Be careful! _ _ _ _ knife I'm holding is sharp.

f. May I introduce you? _ _ _ _ is Mr. and Mrs. Floyd; May I introduce you?
   _ _ _ _ are the Floyds.

g. _ _ _ _ man over there is a doctor; _ _ _ _ men over there are doctors.

h. _ _ _ _ Sunday, when we went for a ride in the car, was wonderful;
   _ _ _ _ Sundays, when went for rides in the car, were wonderful.

i. Let's go out for a meal _ _ _ _ coming Friday; let's go out for a meal one of _ _ _ _ days.

j. _ _ _ _ was a funny thing to say; _ _ _ _ were funny things to say.

Lösung 3: a. he b. they c. him d. it e. him f. her g. it h. they i. it j. her k. we l. him m. us n. it
o. her

3. HIM OR HER Ersetzen Sie das Wort in Klammern durch das richtige Personalpronomen!

a. (Edward) was late for school.

b. (Mary and Connie) passed their driving-test on the same day.

c. Janet loves (Maurice).

d. (The worm) slithered across the damp earth.

e. It was Carrie's turn to bathe (their Alsatian Rex).

f. Ron has bought some flowers for (Janet).

g. "I love (my job)," said the photographer.

h. (The customs officers) searched Tom's bags.

i. Miriam has still got (the record).

j. The jacket belongs to (Denise).

k. (Barbara and I) took a walk on the beach.

l. I handed (Nigel) the documents.

m. She cast a stern glance at (Jake and me).

n. (The dragon) is the first monster to appear in the film.

o. Let's take this to (the seamstress).

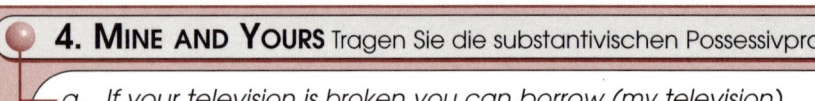

4. MINE AND YOURS Tragen Sie die substantivischen Possessivpronomen ein!

a. *If your television is broken you can borrow (my television).*

b. *Are those trousers (my trousers)?*

c. *We would be happy to lend you (our lawnmower).*

d. *I hope someone buys (my novel).*

e. *Kevin was annoyed because (his football) had a hole in it.*

f. *They repeatedly bragged about (their house).*

g. *Sue drove to work in (my car).*

h. *Our dog can jump over (their fence).*

i. *John flexed his muscles and Gary flexed (his muscles).*

j. *The fox pricked up its ears and the rabbit pricked up (its ears).*

k. *If you ask nicely, they'll let you use (their computer).*

l. *That doesn't belong to you, it's (our family's).*

m. *I'll tell you my phone number if you tell me (your number).*

n. *As he had no hat, he had to borrow (her hat) - the pink one!*

o. *Tell me your thoughts and I'll tell you (my thoughts).*

Lösung 5: a. isn't he? b. mustn't he? c. doesn't he? d. have they? e. mustn't they? f. can they? g. doesn't he? h. didn't I? i. can one? j. won't you? k. shouldn't they? l. mightn't they? m. didn't they? n. wouldn't he? o. can't he?

5. IT'S FUN, ISN'T IT? Ergänzen Sie die Question Tags!

a. Mr. Brady's cousin's a policeman, ... ?

b. He must arrest thieves, ... ?

c. He drives a big police car, ... ?

d. The Walkers haven't got a nice house, ... ?

e. They must move to a new town, ... ?

f. They can't stay in their old house, ... ?

g. The Minister speaks very badly, ... ?

h. I lost all my belongings last night, ... ?

i. One can never be sure, ... ?

j. You will break the news gently to her, ... ?

k. They should be home any second now, ... ?

l. They might get a second chance, ... ?

m. The neighbours made some racket last night, ... ?

n. He would risk his neck to help a friend, ... ?

o. Mr. Carswell can speak three languages, ... ?

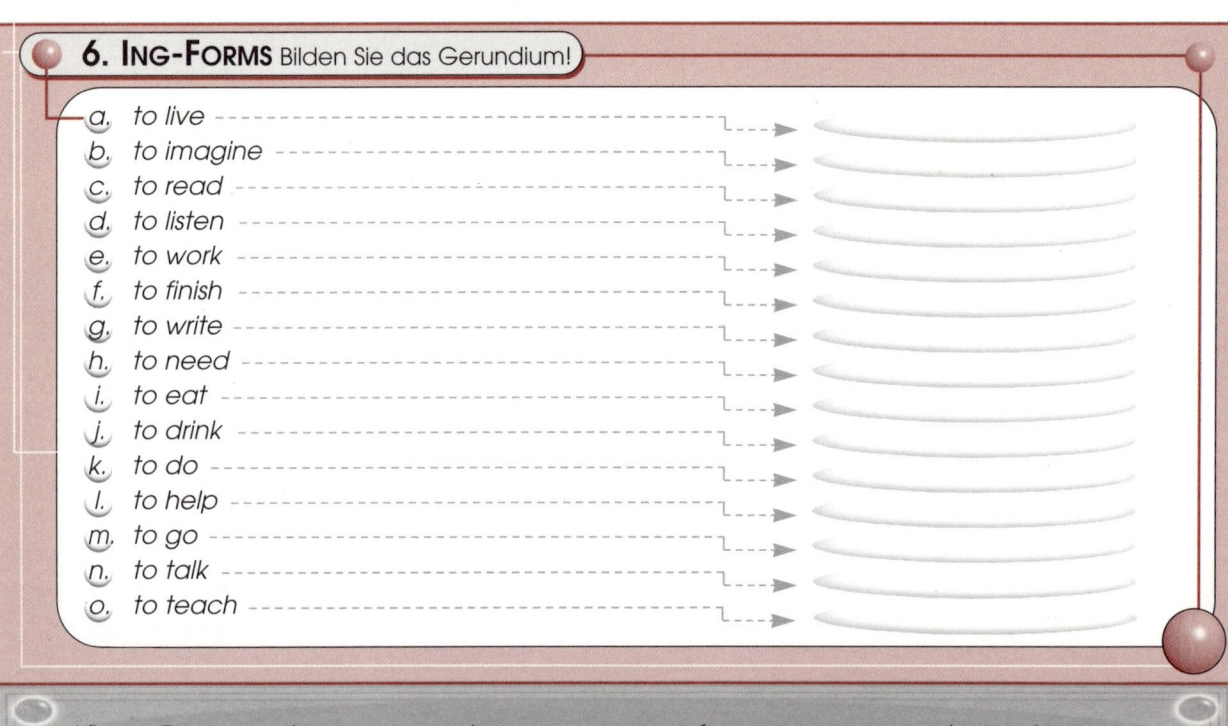

6. ING-FORMS Bilden Sie das Gerundium!

a. to live ------------------------------→
b. to imagine --------------------------→
c. to read -----------------------------→
d. to listen ----------------------------→
e. to work -----------------------------→
f. to finish ----------------------------→
g. to write ----------------------------→
h. to need -----------------------------→
i. to eat -------------------------------→
j. to drink -----------------------------→
k. to do -------------------------------→
l. to help ------------------------------→
m. to go -------------------------------→
n. to talk ------------------------------→
o. to teach ----------------------------→

Lösung 7: a. some b. any c. any d. some; any e. any f. any; some g. some h. any i. any; some
j. some; some k. some; any

7. SOME OR ANY? Welches der beiden Wörter muss hier stehen?

a. I would like _ _ _ _ butter, please.

b. Sorry, we don't have _ _ _ _ butter.

c. You are in luck. You can take _ _ _ _ bus to Streatham.

d. - Have _ _ _ _ potatoes.
   - Sorry, I don't want _ _ _ _.

e. I don't know if we've got _ _ _ _thing for you, sir.

f. Do _ _ _ _ girls in your school play hockey? - _ _ _ _ do.

g. John has _ _ _ _ things to say to you, Mr. Houston.

h. I don't think _ _ _ _ girls play soccer at our school.

i. - Did _ _ _ _body call for me last night?
   - Yes, _ _ _ _body did.

j. - We have _ _ _ _ really delicious honey.
   - If you want, you can have _ _ _ _.

k. - I need _ _ _ _ information about the meeting.
   - I don't have _ _ _ _ idea what you're talking about.

8. SLOWLY BUT SURELY Bilden Sie die Adverbform des Adjektivs!

a. easy -- ►
b. slow -- ►
c. straight ------------------------------------- ►
d. far -- ►
e. nice --- ►
f. shy -- ►
g. public --------------------------------------- ►
h. good -- ►
i. precise -------------------------------------- ►
j. daily --- ►
k. fast -- ►
l. silly -- ►
m. long --- ►
n. true -- ►
o. basic -- ►

Lösung 9: a. in b. because of c. about d. despite/in spite of e. like f. unlike g. according to h. through i. against j. about k. from ... to l. among m. without n. of o. during

9. PREPOSITIONS Ergänzen Sie die Präpositionen!

a. Disraeli became Prime Minister _ _ _ _ _ _ 1874.   **in**

b. My brother was known as "Tiny" _ _ _ _ _ _ his size.   **wegen**

c. There is a documentary on television tonight _ _ _ _ _ _ Namibia.   **über**

d. Mrs. Cotton managed to sing well _ _ _ _ _ _ her nervousness.   **trotz**

e. In the eyes of many Philip looked _ _ _ _ _ _ his grandfather.   **wie**

f. _ _ _ _ _ _ many people in England, Tracy prefers coffee to tea.   **im Gegensatz zu**

g. _ _ _ _ _ _ the weather forecast it's going to snow soon.   **laut**

h. We travelled _ _ _ _ _ _ the Channel Tunnel on the way to London.   **durch**

i. The Opposition is _ _ _ _ _ _ the Government's proposals.   **gegen**

j. The Humber Bridge is _ _ _ _ _ _ a mile long.   **ungefähr**

k. The shop will be closed _ _ _ _ _ _ April _ _ _ _ _ _ July.   **von/bis**

l. You can say what's on your mind, since you're _ _ _ _ _ _ friends.   **unter**

m. Don't go outside _ _ _ _ _ _ taking your umbrella.   **ohne**

n. He acts as if he were the King _ _ _ _ _ _ England.   **von**

o. Mack made some phone calls _ _ _ _ _ _ the intermission.   **während**

10. ALL, EVERY, EACH, MUCH, MANY, BOTH, EITHER, NEITHER Was muss hier stehen?

a. Does she earn _ _ _ _ _ _ _ _ money?

b. I'm afraid that he does not have _ _ _ _ _ _ _ _ time.

c. You can have _ _ _ _ _ _ _ _ of the two holidays but you can't have _ _ _ _ _ _ _ _.

d. Let's see _ _ _ _ _ _ _ _ shows. As far as I know, he hasn't yet seen _ _ _ _ _ _ _ _.

e. _ _ _ _ _ _ _ _ the children in the class were late.

f. These cost 50 pence _ _ _ _ _ _ _ _.

g. _ _ _ _ _ _ _ _ one in England knows the rules of cricket.

h. I don't know him and _ _ _ _ _ _ _ _ do you.

i. Which Hitchcock films have you seen?
   - Not _ _ _ _ _ _ _ _ of them but _ _ _ _ _ _ _ _.

j. Where are Bruce and Joel? I've seen _ _ _ _ _ _ _ _ of them, I'm afraid.

k. Do you know a limerick? Yes, my uncle taught me _ _ _ _ _ _ _ _.

l. A policeman should be alert at _ _ _ _ _ _ _ _ times.

11. COMPLETE THE SENTENCE Ist hier ein Stützwort nötig oder nicht?

a. Both speeches were good, but Paul's was the better _ _ _ _ of the two.

b. That film was boring, but I recently saw a more interesting _ _ _ _

c. The funny _ _ _ _ was that he didn't know that it was all a joke.

d. Nobody except a crazy _ _ _ _ would try that.

e. Your mother was a very kind _ _ _ _.

f. Is your brother the tall man or the short _ _ _ _?

g. Your son Paul is certainly a clever _ _ _ _.

h. The charity provides clothing to the less fortunate _ _ _ _.

i. The group consists of two white men and four black _ _ _ _.

j. I have no money left — do you have any _ _ _ _?

k. The best _ _ _ _ about her plan is its simplicity.

l. I want to start collecting model planes, but so far I only have two _ _ _ _.

m. I like this brand better than any of the other _ _ _ _.

n. Three Irish _ _ _ _ were sitting at the next table.

o. The shop has both cheap items and very expensive _ _ _ _.

12. QUESTIONS Wissen Sie die passenden Interrogativpronomen?

a. To _ _ _ _ _ _ _ _ did you speak?

b. _ _ _ _ _ _ _ _ is your favourite singer?

c. _ _ _ _ _ _ _ _ do you keep in your wallet?

d. _ _ _ _ _ _ _ _ of the two musicals do you prefer?

e. _ _ _ _ _ _ _ _ is that? (Who does it belong to?)

f. _ _ _ _ _ _ _ _ did you say to him?

g. _ _ _ _ _ _ _ _ time is it?

h. _ _ _ _ _ _ _ _ of you want to go to the shops for me?

i. _ _ _ _ _ _ _ _ told you I was ill?

j. _ _ _ _ _ _ _ _ is your new house like?

k. _ _ _ _ _ _ _ _ is the meaning of this?

l. _ _ _ _ _ _ _ _ lives next door to you?

m. _ _ _ _ _ _ _ _ of them is responsible?

n. Go back to the girl _ _ _ _ _ _ _ _ loves you.

o. _ _ _ _ _ _ _ _ glasses are these?

whose
which
what
whom
which one
who
where
when

13. PREPOSITIONS Vervollständigen Sie die Sätze!

a.	Elizabeth wondered _ _ _ the birds went in winter.	wohin
b.	_ _ _ she finds out about it, she'll be angry.	wenn
c.	_ _ _ everyone had met her, no one knew her very well.	obwohl
d.	_ _ _ keep fit, he jogs every morning.	um
e.	Throughout the lecture, Deborah looked _ _ _ she were about to fall asleep.	als ob
f.	Grace always felt tired _ _ _ Jill hardly ever slept.	während
g.	_ _ _ George phones, you can tell him that I'll call him back.	wenn/falls
h.	This year Thomas has cultivated more potatoes _ _ _ he can eat himself.	als
i.	He had _ _ _ a long time to wait _ _ _ he decided to leave.	so/dass
j.	Christopher couldn't swim _ _ _ his life depended on it.	selbst wenn
k.	Victor wanted to buy a new pair of shoes _ _ _ he couldn't find one.	aber

14. IT'S EASY, ISN'T IT? Wie lauten die Question Tags?

a. Mike's clothes are in his suitcase, ... ?
b. Your nephew has a car of his own, ... ?
c. Ray had never been to Italy before, ... ?
d. Richard could have been successful in any profession, ... ?
e. Pat has had many problems with his new computer, ... ?
f. Shawn claims that Elvis is still alive, ... ?
g. Her grandparents own eighty acres of land, ... ?
h. Her uncle collects rare coins, ... ?
i. The exam was more difficult than anyone expected, ... ?
j. The weather is nice today, ... ?
k. You're a friend of Bob's, ... ?
l. He's not busy, ... ?
m. Sarah's going to talk to her husband, ... ?
n. He does impressions of celebrities, ... ?
o. They're expecting their second child, ... ?

Lösung 15: a. holiday b. the house; the keys c. the car d. Regent Street e. the radio
f. the Eiffel Tower g. the Thames h. the Netherlands i. good old John j. the English Channel
k. dinner l. school m. the city n. the Millers o. church

Lösung 14: a. aren't they? b. doesn't he? c. had he? d. couldn't he? e. hasn't he?
f. doesn't he? g. don't they? h. doesn't he? i. wasn't it? j. isn't it? k. aren't you? l. is he?
m. isn't she? n. doesn't he? o. aren't they?

15. SOMETHING WRONG? Muss der bestimmte Artikel stehen oder nicht?

a. Today we are going on _ _ _ _ _ _ holiday.

b. We locked up _ _ _ _ _ _ house and gave _ _ _ _ _ _ keys to our neighbour.

c. Tommy, our dog, sprang into _ _ _ _ _ _ car.

d. We drove along _ _ _ _ _ _ Regent Street.

e. Mother switched on _ _ _ _ _ _ radio.

f. During our trip to Paris we were on top of _ _ _ _ _ _ Eiffel Tower.

g. After an hour we crossed _ _ _ _ _ _ Thames.

h. We were on our way to _ _ _ _ _ _ Netherlands.

i. I was looking forward to seeing _ _ _ _ _ _ good old John again.

j. As we crossed _ _ _ _ _ _ English Channel it began to rain.

k. We decided it was time to eat _ _ _ _ _ _ dinner.

l. I was glad that I did not have to be in _ _ _ _ _ _ school.

m. We spent two weeks in _ _ _ _ _ _ city of Rome before returning home.

n. Our neighbours, _ _ _ _ _ _ Millers, greeted us.

o. Father went to _ _ _ _ _ _ church the next day.

16. MORE THAN ONE Wie lautet der Plural dieser Wörter?

a. Look at the beautiful _ _ _ _ _ _ _ over there!
b. You can keep the _ _ _ _ _ _ _.
c. Would you like to see our beautiful _ _ _ _ _ _ _?
d. Where did you put the _ _ _ _ _ _ _?
e. Have you seen our _ _ _ _ _ _ _?
f. I am going to hang the _ _ _ _ _ _ _ above the fireplace.
g. Have you fed the _ _ _ _ _ _ _ yet?
h. We all admired the returning _ _ _ _ _ _ _.
i. Harry gave the _ _ _ _ _ _ _ five pounds.
j. Julia carefully put the _ _ _ _ _ _ _ back into the water.
k. I think you are using the wrong _ _ _ _ _ _ _.
l. Have you completed your _ _ _ _ _ _ _ yet?
m. I'm going to speak to the _ _ _ _ _ _ _.
n. Don't stamp on my _ _ _ _ _ _ _.
o. Why is Derek hiding in the _ _ _ _ _ _ _?

tree
box
church
dictionary
sheep
picture
calf
hero
child
cod
criterion
inquiry
boss
foot
bush

Lösung 17: a. I'm not b. Weren't we? c. Wasn't I? d. You aren't/You're not e. She isn't/She's not
f. I won't g. They don't h. You can't i. Isn't it? j. Aren't they? k. Didn't he? l. Doesn't she?
m. We don't n. She can't o. Aren't you?

17. JUST SAY NO Geben Sie die verneinte Form an!

a. I am. ----------->
b. Were we? ----------->
c. Was I? ----------->
d. You are. ----------->
e. She is. ----------->
f. I will. ----------->
g. They do. ----------->
h. You can. ----------->
i. Is it? ----------->
j. Are they? ----------->
k. Did he? ----------->
l. Does she? ----------->
m. We do. ----------->
n. She can. ----------->
o. Are you? ----------->

18. UP AND AWAY Setzen Sie Präposition oder Adverb ein!

a. The Browns made _ _ _ _ _ after their fight.
b. Could you please pay _ _ _ _ _ the money you owe me?
c. I would like to take a day _ _ _ _ _ next week.
d. I'm really fed _ _ _ _ _ _ _ _ _ _ this weather.
e. How do you put _ _ _ _ _ _ _ _ _ _ the noise from the road?
f. Oh, no. We've run _ _ _ _ _ _ _ _ _ _ milk. Can you go and get some more?
g. You must learn to face _ _ _ _ _ _ _ _ _ _ the problem.
h. Are you _ _ _ _ _ to going out this evening, or are you feeling too tired?
i. Don't go back _ _ _ _ _ your promise!
j. He always stands _ _ _ _ _ _ _ _ _ _ his little sister when she has problems.
k. What did you do that _ _ _ _ _? That was stupid!
l. We're behind three goals to one, but it's not _ _ _ _ _ yet.
m. I can do _ _ _ _ _ your snappy remarks!
n. Brett's the kind of person you can rely _ _ _ _ _.
o. Could I have a piece _ _ _ _ _ that pie?

Lösung 19: a. Do we love? b. Do they work? c. Do I drink? d. Does it sleep? e. Do you wait?
f. Does she sit? g. Does she have it? h. Is it good? i. Can we? j. Do I? k. Do they rest? l. Do I see?
m. Does John do it? n. Does she leave? o. Did we leave?

19. ANY QUESTIONS? Bilden Sie Fragen!

a. We love................... ?
b. They work .... ?
c. I drink...................... ?
d. It sleeps................... ?
e. You wait................ ?
f. She sits.................... ?
g. She has it .... ?
h. It's good .... ?
i. We can................... ?
j. I do......................... ?
k. They rest................. ?
l. I see....................... ?
m. John does it.......... ?
n. She leaves............. ?
o. We left.................... ?

20. ARTICLE OR NO ARTICLE? Wo muss der unbestimmte Artikel stehen?

a. The police are still looking for _ _ _ _ _ _ evidence.
b. Mrs. Marcus admitted to having _ _ _ _ _ _ fascination for auto racing.
c. Colin attended pottery classes twice _ _ _ _ _ _ week.
d. Cordelia could feel _ _ _ _ _ _ sand in her shoes.
e. What would you like for _ _ _ _ _ _ breakfast, sir?
f. Paul wants to be _ _ _ _ _ _ accountant.
g. Do you have _ _ _ _ _ _ money?
h. Mary leads _ _ _ _ _ _ happy life.
i. To speak in public requires _ _ _ _ _ _ _ _ _ _ _ _ special kind of courage.
j. Jean puts _ _ _ _ _ _ make-up on every morning.
k. Anne is _ _ _ _ _ _ member of the Bridge Club.
l. This fingerprint is _ _ _ _ _ _ proof that he did it.
m. Make _ _ _ _ _ _ wish and maybe it'll come true.
n. Here's _ _ _ _ _ _ present - open it right away!
o. Andy wants _ _ _ _ _ _ answer, and he wants it now!

Lösung 21: a. am b. do c. will d. can e. would f. aren't g. won't h. didn't i. couldn't j. aren't
k. does l. isn't m. doesn't n. has o. didn't

21. QUESTIONS AND ANSWERS Setzen Sie das passende Wort ein!

a.	Are you Spanish?	a.	Yes, I_____
b.	Do you like cricket?	b.	Yes, I_____
c.	Will he stay?	c.	Yes, he_____
d.	Can They speak English?	d.	Yes, they_____
e.	Would you like some tea?	e.	Yes, I_____
f.	Are they British?	f.	No, they_____
g.	Will you see him tomorrow?	g.	No, I_____
h.	Did she use to live here?	h.	No, she_____
i.	Could they swim?	i.	No, they_____
j.	Are we rich?	j.	No, you_____
k.	Does he drive a sports car?	k.	Yes, he_____
l.	Is Mars farther away than Saturn?	l.	No, it_____
m.	Does Bob have a licence?	m.	No, he_____
n.	Has the train arrived yet?	n.	Yes, it_____
o.	Did he have fun?	o.	No, he_____

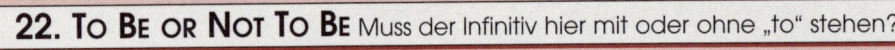

22. TO BE OR NOT TO BE Muss der Infinitiv hier mit oder ohne „to" stehen?

a. There was nothing else **do/to do** but go home.

b. Why not **stay/to stay**?

c. We want you **come/to come**.

d. I'm learning **speak/to speak** French at the moment.

e. We heard him **play/to play** the piano.

f. She knows how **repair/to repair** computers.

g. We went to school in order **learn/to learn**.

h. I would rather **read/to read** than work.

i. He made us **do/to do** the dishes.

j. These goods are easy **sell/to sell**.

k. There are many things **do/to do**.

l. We watched her **run/to run** the race.

m. They seem **like/to like** him.

n. Please bring me something **read/to read**.

o. They are always the last **arrive/to arrive**.

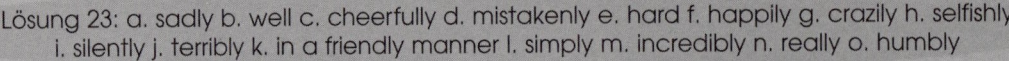

Lösung 23: a. sadly b. well c. cheerfully d. mistakenly e. hard f. happily g. crazily h. selfishly i. silently j. terribly k. in a friendly manner l. simply m. incredibly n. really o. humbly

Lösung 22: a. to do b. stay c. to come d. to speak e. play f. to repair g. to learn h. read i. do
j. to sell k. to do l. run m. to like n. to read o. to arrive

23. ADVERBS Bilden Sie die Adverbien!

a. sad --- ▷

b. good --- ▷

c. cheerful --- ▷

d. mistaken --- ▷

e. hard --- ▷

f. happy --- ▷

g. crazy --- ▷

h. selfish --- ▷

i. silent --- ▷

j. terrible --- ▷

k. friendly --- ▷

l. simple --- ▷

m. incredible --- ▷

n. real --- ▷

o. humble --- ▷

24. IT'S EASY, ISN'T IT? Ergänzen Sie folgende Aussagen mit Question Tags!

a. They like ice-cream, ... ?
b. She swims every morning, ... ?
c. He didn't see us, ... ?
d. They spoke to you, ... ?
e. She didn't have to wait long, ... ?
f. She invited you, ... ?
g. You don't have a calculator, ... ?
h. They knew his address, ... ?
i. You love me, ... ?
j. You couldn't imagine such a thing, ... ?
k. Eric doesn't like chocolate, ... ?
l. You like dogs, ... ?
m. It's a bit annoying, ... ?
n. I can't help it, ... ?
o. Karen's an old friend of yours, ... ?

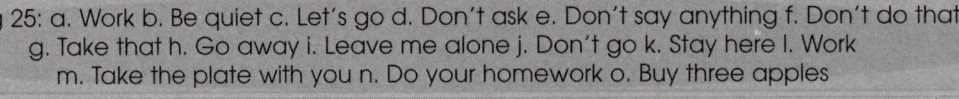

Lösung 25: a. Work b. Be quiet c. Let's go d. Don't ask e. Don't say anything f. Don't do that
g. Take that h. Go away i. Leave me alone j. Don't go k. Stay here l. Work
m. Take the plate with you n. Do your homework o. Buy three apples

Lösung 24: a. don't they? b. doesn't she? c. did he? d. didn't they? e. did she? f. didn't she?
g. do you? h. didn't they? i. don't you? j. could you? k. does he? l. don't you? m. isn't it?
n. can I? p. isn't she?

25. IMPERATIVE Übersetzen Sie die Befehlsformen!

a. Arbeite! .... !
b. Seid ruhig! .... !
c. Gehen wir! .... !
d. Frag nicht! .... !
e. Sag nichts! .... !
f. Tu das nicht! .... !
g. Nimm das! .... !
h. Geh weg! .... !
i. Lass mich in Ruhe! .... !
j. Geh nicht! .... !
k. Bleibt hier! .... !
l. Arbeitet! .... !
m. Nehmen Sie den Teller mit! .... !
n. Macht eure Hausaufgaben! .... !
o. Kaufe drei Äpfel! .... !

26. IN, AT, ON, TO, DURING, BEFORE Setzen Sie die richtige Präposition ein!

a. In Bavaria children start school _ _ _ _ the age of six.

b. Christine and Steve were married _ _ _ _ Friday.

c. He suffered a broken leg _ _ _ _ the Battle of the Somme.

d. The first modern Olympic Games took place _ _ _ _ the 19th century.

e. Peter started working for the company _ _ _ _ 1998.

f. I go home to England _ _ _ _ Christmas.

g. In the summer we sit on the balcony _ _ _ _ night and drink wine.

h. We usually go dancing _ _ _ _ Tuesday.

i. Pat is an economist but he has no job _ _ _ _ the moment.

j. The house was small so we got it built _ _ _ _ a week.

k. In Britain cricket is played _ _ _ _ the summer.

l. John and I were at school _ _ _ _ the same time.

m. I did my driving test _ _ _ _ a Monday.

n. The band was formed _ _ _ _ the late 1990s.

o. Mary had her first child _ _ _ _ 18.

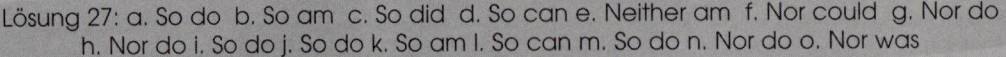

Lösung 27: a. So do b. So am c. So did d. So can e. Neither am f. Nor could g. Nor do
h. Nor do i. So do j. So do k. So am l. So can m. So do n. Nor do o. Nor was

27. DO YOU AGREE? Stimmen Sie den Aussagen zu!

a. I love cats. .... I. __

b. He's English. .... I. __

c. We saw him last week. .... I. __

d. We can speak English. .... I. __

e. He isn't Spanish. .... I. __

f. She couldn't swim. .... I. __

g. We don't like her. .... I. __

h. I don't enjoy skiing. .... I. __

i. Mark means what he says. .... I. __

j. I get pimples when I eat chocolate. ...... I. __

k. Mick's popular with women. .... I. __

l. She can water-ski. .... I. __

m. Beth has three children. .... I. __

n. I don't like the sound of it. .... I. __

o. He wasn't a very good student. .... I. __

28. MYSELF, YOURSELF, HERSELF Setzen Sie die passenden Reflexivpronomen ein!

a. Who taught Dave how to play the bagpipes? Nobody, he taught _ _ _ _ _ _ _ _

b. Shall I pour the wine? No, I'll do it _ _ _ _ _ _ _ _

c. Have you heard the news? Yes, I can hardly believe it _ _ _ _ _ _ _ _

d. Will we tell Peter and Janet? No. Let them find out for _ _ _ _ _ _ _ _

e. Who will take us to the train? We'll have to get there _ _ _ _ _ _ _ _

f. Can you get the paper for us? Why don't you fetch it _ _ _ _ _ _ _ _

g. Does the headmaster have a house help ? No, he does everything _ _ _ _ _ _ _ _

h. Can we have some beer? Help _ _ _ _ _ _ _ _

i. Will we get Tom to fix the bike? Let's do it _ _ _ _ _ _ _ _

j. Who made Irene's jacket? She did it _ _ _ _ _ _ _ _

k. If you want something done right, do it _ _ _ _ _ _ _ _.

l. Bud's always scratching _ _ _ _ _ _ _ _ - he hasn't showered in quite a while.

m. I know that you two are engaged - you told me so _ _ _ _ _ _ _ _.

n. I helped _ _ _ _ _ _ _ _ to a big serving.

o. The award was presented by none other than the President _ _ _ _ _ _ _ _.

Lösung 29: a. bushes b. teeth c. holidays d. peaches e. radios f. knives g. tomatoes h. children
i. winters j. oxen k. wives l. matches m. pianos n. halves o. babies

29. ONE MAN - TWO MEN Kennen Sie den Plural dieser Wörter?

a. bush --------------------------- ⟶
b. tooth --------------------------- ⟶
c. holiday --------------------------- ⟶
d. peach --------------------------- ⟶
e. radio --------------------------- ⟶
f. knife --------------------------- ⟶
g. tomato --------------------------- ⟶
h. child --------------------------- ⟶
i. winter --------------------------- ⟶
j. ox --------------------------- ⟶
k. wife --------------------------- ⟶
l. match --------------------------- ⟶
m. piano --------------------------- ⟶
n. half --------------------------- ⟶
o. baby --------------------------- ⟶

30. SOME OR ANY? Setzen Sie „some", „any" oder ihre Zusammensetzungen ein!

a. Have you got _ _ _ _ _ old clothes for the Red Cross?

b. There is _ _ _ _ _ standing at the door.

c. You can change your money into English pounds at _ _ _ _ _ bank.

d. Did you buy _ _ _ _ _ in the sales?

e. "Would you like _ _ _ _ _ sugar?"

f. "Hello, is _ _ _ _ _ there?"

g. If _ _ _ _ _ would like to take a sample home, please do so.

h. I will forward _ _ _ _ _ post to your new address.

i. _ _ _ _ _ has forgotten his scarf.

j. I'd go _ _ _ _ _ but Brazil on my holidays.

k. Can you send me _ _ _ _ _ leaflets on local festivals?

l. "What would you like for Christmas?" "_ _ _ _ _, I don't care."

m. You can travel _ _ _ _ _ day you like except Sunday.

n. "Does _ _ _ _ _ mind if I open the window"

o. _ _ _ _ _ people are terribly lazy.

31. QUESTION TAGS Vervollständigen Sie die Fragen!

a. You're British, ... ?
b. We can swim, ... ?
c. They aren't happy, ... ?
d. Your father's a teacher, ... ?
e. She wouldn't like a beer, ... ?
f. You've seen her, ... ?
g. They can't come, ... ?
h. He's working tonight, ... ?
i. He's French, ... ?
j. They won't ring, ... ?
k. She isn't here, ... ?
l. He'll pay, ... ?
m. You would like that, ... ?
n. She wasn't here yesterday, ... ?
o. They couldn't find your number, ... ?

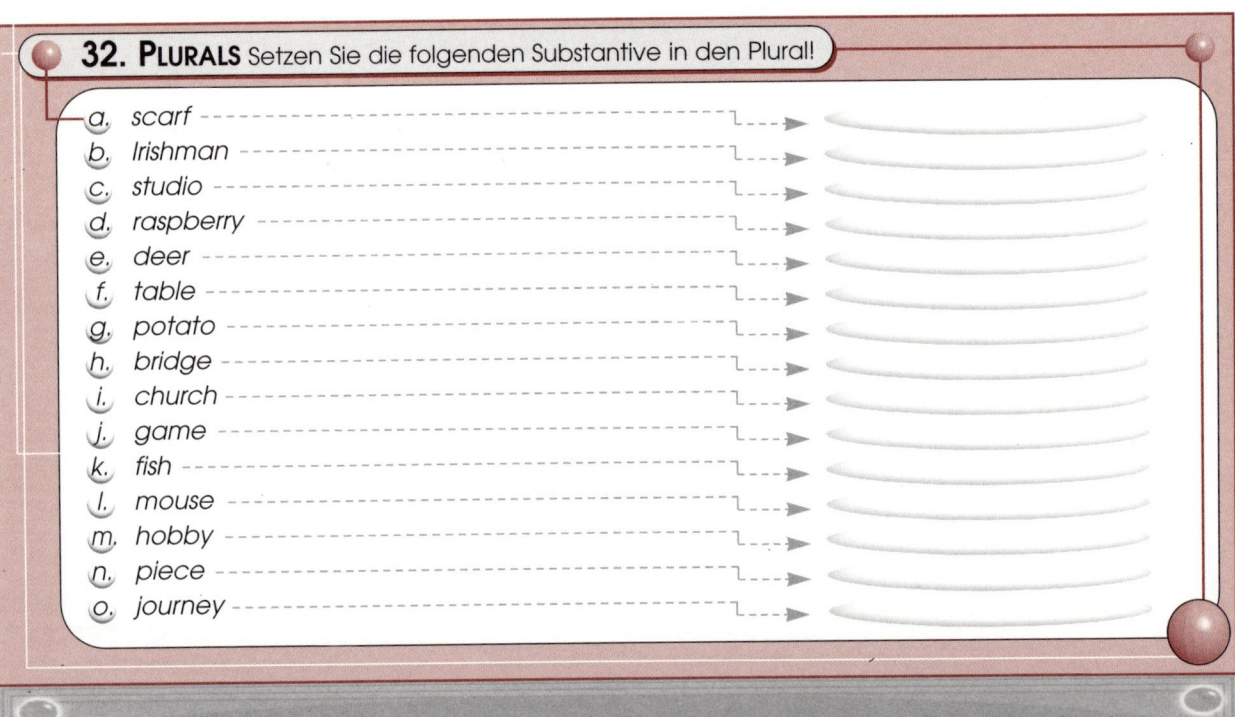

32. PLURALS Setzen Sie die folgenden Substantive in den Plural!

a. scarf ----------------------------------▸
b. Irishman -------------------------------▸
c. studio ---------------------------------▸
d. raspberry ------------------------------▸
e. deer -----------------------------------▸
f. table -----------------------------------▸
g. potato ---------------------------------▸
h. bridge ---------------------------------▸
i. church ---------------------------------▸
j. game -----------------------------------▸
k. fish ------------------------------------▸
l. mouse ----------------------------------▸
m. hobby ---------------------------------▸
n. piece -----------------------------------▸
o. journey --------------------------------▸

Lösung 33: a. to; at; on b. at c. on; next to d. at e. into; to f. at; to; in; out of g. until/before h. on
i. to j. from k. at; to l. to; for m. at; in n. at

33. A SHORT STORY Setzen Sie die richtige Präposition ein!

a. When he went _ _ _ _ bed _ _ _ _ night _ _ _ _ Sunday the first of April, James was excited.

b. Tomorrow would be his first day _ _ _ _ school.

c. He had placed all his clothes _ _ _ the table _ _ _ _ his bed.

d. He looked across _ _ _ _ his backpack which was packed and ready.

e. Jumping _ _ _ _ bed he said good night _ _ _ _ his mother.

f. When the alarm clock rang _ _ _ _ quarter _ _ _ _ seven _ _ _ _ the morning he sprang
_ _ _ _ _ _ _ the bed.

g. It wasn't long _ _ _ _ he was ready.

h. After he had finished his breakfast his mother helped him put _ _ _ _ his coat.

i. Together the two of them walked _ _ _ _ school.

j. _ _ _ _ time to time James saw other children with their parents.

k. When they arrived _ _ _ _ the school James's mother took him _ _ _ _ the classroom.

l. His mother spoke _ _ _ _ the teacher _ _ _ _ a few minutes and then she said goodbye.

m. James sat _ _ _ _ a desk _ _ _ _ the middle of the room.

n. The teacher smiled _ _ _ _ the class and began to teach.

34. QUESTION TAGS Vervollständigen Sie die Fragen. Verwenden Sie Formen von "to do"!

a. They look after their children well, ... ?

b. You spoke English as a child, ... ?

c. He works for a Scottish firm, ... ?

d. Caesar died in Rome, ... ?

e. He doesn't drink, ... ?

f. You don't mind if I smoke, ... ?

g. She found her pen, ... ?

h. Susan doesn't play the piano well, ... ?

i. She dresses prettily, ... ?

j. The house looks beautiful, ... ?

k. You attended Eton, ... ?

l. Shannon loves to jog, ... ?

m. Jeff prefers beer to root beer, ... ?

n. Your parents paid you a visit, ... ?

o. Jake does karate, ... ?

Lösung 35: a. modern architecture b. the afternoon c. bus d. Regent's Park e. life f. the sun
g. advice; information h. Sunday mornings; bed i. ham; supper j. the clothes; the day
k. the television l. literature; philosophy; television m. Swedes n. work o. Love

Lösung 34: a. don't they? b. didn't you? c. doesn't he? d. didn't he? e. does he? f. do you?
g. didn't she? h. does she? i. doesn't she? j. doesn't it? k. didn't you? l. doesn't she?
m. doesn't he? n. didn't they? o. doesn't he?

35. "LOVE" OR "THE LOVE"? Bestimmter Artikel: Ja oder Nein?

a. My sister has always been fascinated by _ _ _ _ _ _ _ _ _ _ _ modern architecture.

b. In _ _ _ _ _ _ afternoon we went sightseeing.

c. We went by _ _ _ _ _ _ bus to Oxford Circus.

d. I took a stroll in _ _ _ _ _ _ Regent's Park.

e. In those days, _ _ _ _ _ _ life seemed so easy.

f. I saw my friend Paul. He was sitting back enjoying _ _ _ _ _ _sun on his face.

g. Later he asked me for _ _ _ _ _ _advice and _ _ _ _ _ _information.

h. He asked whether it was unhealthy to spend _ _ _ _ _ _Sunday mornings in _ _ _ _ _ _ bed.

i. That evening, we had _ _ _ _ _ _ ham for _ _ _ _ _ _ supper.

j. Mother showed Julia _ _ _ _ _ _ clothes she had bought _ _ _ _ _ _day before.

k. Father switched on _ _ _ _ _ _television to watch sports.

l. He likes _ _ _ _ _ _ literature and _ _ _ _ _ _philosophy, she likes _ _ _ _ _ _television.

m. Are the two _ _ _ _ _ _Swedes who were here yesterday coming back?

n. I have one on my desk at _ _ _ _ _ _work.

o. _ _ _ _ _ _Love works in mysterious ways.

36. WHICH, WHOM, WHAT, THAT ETC. Setzen Sie das Relativpronomen ein!

a. I bought the cowboy boots in Austin, _ _ _ _ _ is the capital of Texas.
b. You ought to meet Gloria, _ _ _ _ _ lives next door.
c. His fountain pen, _ _ _ _ _ is a valuable family heirloom, is very dear to him.
d. Cary really embarrassed himself, _ _ _ _ _ really isn't too surprising.
e. Heather, _ _ _ _ _ father is a multimillionaire, is known for being a snob.
f. Bruno, _ _ _ _ _ I owe two hundred dollars, wants his money back.
g. I think I understand _ _ _ _ _ you're saying - you don't like him very much.
h. That was the greatest hockey game _ _ _ _ _ I have ever seen.
i. My friend Don, _ _ _ _ _ was at my wedding, is coming to tea.
j. Our headmaster, _ _ _ _ _ car broke down last week, bought a new one.
k. My brother, _ _ _ _ _ I explained our homework, is a fantastic footballer.
l. Our old accordion, _ _ _ _ _ has lost a few keys and buttons, will be repaired.
m. Widow Cassidy, _ _ _ _ _ husband died ten years ago, is to marry again.
n. Mr. Collins, _ _ _ _ _ you spoke yesterday, is a friend of mine.
o. Kevin, _ _ _ _ _ came back to England last week, had been away for two years.

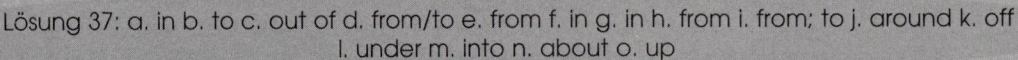

Lösung 37: a. in b. to c. out of d. from/to e. from f. in g. in h. from i. from; to j. around k. off l. under m. into n. about o. up

37. OUT AND ABOUT Setzen Sie die richtige Präposition ein!

a. My father has taken a job _ _ _ _ India.

b. We will be moving _ _ _ _ Bombay soon.

c. Kerry took a bottle of cooking oil _ _ _ _ the fridge.

d. While walking _ _ _ _ his house _ _ _ _ the school he slipped three times.

e. The bus leaves for London _ _ _ _ the bus-stop across the road.

f. He retired as headmaster and bought a house _ _ _ _ the country.

g. Tom is still waiting _ _ _ _ the queue.

h. He knocked the cup _ _ _ _ the table.

i. The buckets of water were passed _ _ _ _ person _ _ _ _ person.

j. Colin and his friends danced _ _ _ _ the maypole.

k. Karl and Jean got _ _ _ _ the train in Cambridge.

l. She noticed a little mouse on the floor _ _ _ _ the chair.

m. It was a half an hour before she went back _ _ _ _ the room.

n. Don't lie _ _ _ _ doing nothing.

o. Get _ _ _ _ and get working.

about
in
at
on
to
into
out (of)
from
off
around
towards
under

38. "A Doctor" or "Doctor"? Muss der unbestimmte Artikel hier stehen oder nicht?

a. Laura is _ _ _ _ _ _ _ _ _ doctor.

b. Mr. Archibald is _ _ _ _ _ _ _ _ _ President of the Cricket Club.

c. As _ _ _ _ _ _ _ _ _ Methodist, Albert loved Wesley's hymns.

d. He has always wanted to live in _ _ _ _ _ _ _ _ _ cottage.

e. Kate lives in _ _ _ _ _ _ _ _ village called Hunstanton.

f. Every Friday there is _ _ _ _ _ _ _ _ _ market on the square.

g. Mr. McLaren is _ _ _ _ _ _ _ _ _ Scotsman.

h. Tripe is considered _ _ _ _ _ _ _ _ _ delicacy in Lyons.

i. His enemies tried to portray him as _ _ _ _ _ _ _ _ _ coward.

j. Every Saturday we buy _ _ _ _ _ _ _ _ _ bread.

k. Last week we had _ _ _ _ _ _ _ _ _ very strange weather.

l. While reading the paper, Teresa saw _ _ _ _ _ _ _ _ _ item of news which interested her.

m. To his dismay, Tom noticed _ _ _ _ _ _ _ _ _ fly in his soup.

n. Normally Mr. Peacock eats _ _ _ _ _ _ _ _ _ light lunch.

o. Mrs. Quincey is _ _ _ _ _ _ _ _ _ author.

Lösung 39: a. can b. is c. is d. haven't e. didn't f. aren't g. do h. isn't i. is j. does k. does l. isn't m. did n. didn't o. did

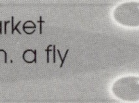

Lösung 38: a. a doctor b. President c. a Methodist d. a cottage e. a village f. a market
g. a Scotsman h. a delicacy i. a coward j. bread k. very strange weather l. an item m. a fly
n. a light lunch o. an author

39. YOU'RE RIGHT Bekräftigen Sie die folgenden Aussagen!

a. They can swim well.
b. They weather is lovely today.
c. Today is Monday.
d. We haven't done it yet.
e. He didn't buy this house.
f. We aren't rich.
g. They like me.
h. The coffee isn't good.
i. That picture frame is a bit crooked.
j. Her face seems familiar.
k. It looks pretty serious.
l. That's not very realistic.
m. Simon memorized the names.
n. I didn't do anything!
o. We did the best we could.

a. Yes, they _____
b. Yes, it _____
c. Yes, it _____
d. No, we _____
e. No, he _____
f. No, we _____
g. Yes, they _____
h. No, it _____
i. Yes, it _____
j. Yes, it _____
k. Yes, it _____
l. No, it _____
m. Yes, he _____
n. No, you _____
o. Yes, we _____

40. WHO, WHICH, WHOSE, WHOM, THAT Setzen Sie die Relativpronomen ein!

a. Suzanne is a nanny _ _ _ _ lives with her employers.

b. The automobile _ _ _ _ you are driving is registered as stolen.

c. The boxer _ _ _ _ won was called "Bonecrusher".

d. I discovered the old photos _ _ _ _ I had been looking for in the attic.

e. Mr. Smith, _ _ _ _ this book belongs, is a librarian.

f. Helen is the first woman _ _ _ _ ever struck me.

g. The advertisement _ _ _ _ you have just seen was brought to you by Waterford Glass Ltd.

h. The boy _ _ _ _ mother has just moved here is named Joey.

i. Wasn't that the boy _ _ _ _ asked you for a date?

j. The fly _ _ _ _ had been annoying me has left.

k. Dr. Reilly is the dentist _ _ _ _ _ _ _ _ most people go to.

l. The theatre, _ _ _ _ _ _ _ _ actors describe as very poor, has many plays on show.

m. I don't know anyone _ _ _ _ the theatre does not fascinate.

n. The school _ _ _ _ _ _ _ _ pupils went to the theatre last Friday is well-known.

o. They sung a song _ _ _ _ _ _ _ _ was very famous.

Lösung 41: a. hasn't she? b. isn't he? c. doesn't he? d. does he? e. doesn't he? f. isn't he?
g. didn't he h. weren't they i. didn't he? j. wasn't she? k. isn't she? l. haven't they?
m. can't they? n. can't he? o. do they?

41. QUESTION TAGS Vervollständigen Sie die Fragen!

a. Jennifer's got a jealous boyfriend, ... ?
b. Kevin is very disappointed about his results, ... ?
c. On the afternoon of the match he gets very anxious, ... ?
d. When they win he doesn't seem sad, ... ?
e. Jerry follows Tom everywhere, ... ?
f. He's the most wonderful tom-cat in the world, ... ?
g. One day, he ran after Lucy, ... ?
h. They were both very lucky not to be injured, ... ?
i. He arrived at the bus stop, ... ?
j. She was quite angry with him, ... ?
k. Mrs. Freeman is a very nosey woman, ... ?
l. The Smiths have got lovely neighbours, ... ?
m. They can talk to them very nicely, ... ?
n. He can juggle, ... ?
o. They don't steal things, ... ?

42. FILL IN THE BLANK Setzen Sie die Präposition oder das Adverb ein!

a. The thief broke _ _ _ _ _ the house and stole some jewellery.
b. I'll look _ _ _ _ _ the problem as soon as possible.
c. He was happy to run _ _ _ _ _ his old girlfriend after so many years.
d. You take _ _ _ _ _ your father: you both have the same eyes.
e. We are very happy that our old cat and the new puppy get _ _ _ _ _ so well.
f. I'm trying to break _ _ _ _ _ these new penny loafers.
g. His son is very cheeky and always answers _ _ _ _ _ at school.
h. I was sick last week. I hope I can catch _ _ _ _ _ on all that work.
i. Don't give _ _ _ _ _! Keep trying!
j. Can you hold _ _ _ _ _ a minute? I just have to answer the phone.
k. Do you mind if I ring _ _ _ _ _ my mother?
l. His grandparents brought him _ _ _ _ _.
m. They called their wedding _ _ _ _ _ at the last minute.
n. Please try to give _ _ _ _ _ smoking!
o. I'm very disappointed that he let her _ _ _ _ _ again.

Lösung 43: a. belongs b. am thinking c. hates d. looks e. do you think; he is thinking
f. believe g. know h. Do you like i. is waiting; seems j. is rehearsing; sounds k. am having
l. am reading m. knows n. is studying o. is behaving

Lösung 42: a. into b. at c. into d. after e. along f. in g. back h. up i. up j. on k. up l. up m. off n. up o. down

43. SIMPLE PRESENT OR PRESENT CONTINUOUS? Setzen Sie die richtige Verbform ein!

a. It _ _ _ _ to a rare group of plants. — **belong**

b. I _ _ _ _ of visiting my parents tomorrow. — **think**

c. Sharon _ _ _ _ goldfish. — **hate**

d. Simon _ _ _ _ worried. — **look**

e. What _ _ _ _ _ _ _ _ about? — **you/think**

f. We _ _ _ _ in God. — **believe**

g. I _ _ _ _ what you mean. — **know**

h. _ _ _ _ rap music? — **you/like**

i. A man _ _ _ _ in the hall. He _ _ _ _ to know you. — **wait; seem**

j. She _ _ _ _ at present. Her new song _ _ _ _ lovely. — **rehearse; sound**

k. I _ _ _ _ lunch right now - may I call you back? — **have**

l. This week I _ _ _ _ a great book about the Knights of the Round Table. — **read**

m. Sarah _ _ _ _ an old man who does great magic tricks. — **know**

n. Phil _ _ _ _ for an exam - don't disturb him! — **study**

o. My godfather _ _ _ _ rudely these days. — **behave**

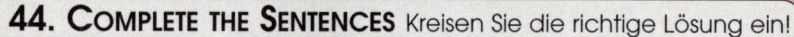

44. COMPLETE THE SENTENCES Kreisen Sie die richtige Lösung ein!

a. What **were you doing/do you do** when the sun came up?

b. What **are/does** your favourite hobbies?

c. **Have you ever read/Do you ever read** Romeo and Juliet?

d. What **are you do/do you do**?

e. How often **is/does** he visit you?

f. He visits us once **a week/the week**.

g. We **used to/are used to** have an account at this bank.

h. What where you doing when the bus **stopped/was stopping**?

i. This road is **straight/straightly**.

j. **He's usually working/He usually works** at home.

k. She speaks English very **well/good**.

l. How much **cost this/does this cost**?

m. After the pub, we **have gone/went** home.

n. What **do you do/are you doing** at the moment?

o. Yesterday he **drives/drove** home.

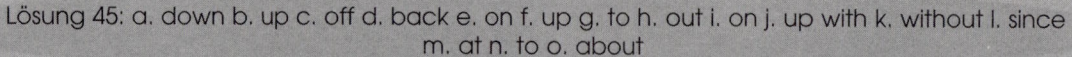

Lösung 45: a. down b. up c. off d. back e. on f. up g. to h. out i. on j. up with k. without l. since m. at n. to o. about

45. ONWARD AND UPWARD Setzen Sie die passenden Präpositionen ein!

a. I was really disappointed when she let me _ _ _ _ _ after all her promises.

b. Last week all the cars were held _ _ _ _ _ by the police because of a search.

c. The plane will take _ _ _ _ _ in five minutes.

d. My children keep answering _ _ _ _ _ every time I tell them to do something!

e. Whenever the postman opened the gate, the vicious dog turned _ _ _ _ _ him.

f. I didn't remember her number and had to look it _ _ _ _ _ in the phone book.

g. The patient was slowly coming _ _ _ _ _ after the operation.

h. These exercises are really difficult, I can't make _ _ _ _ _ how to fill in all those gaps!

i. Granny needn't try _ _ _ _ _ this coat, it's far too long for her.

j. You wouldn't believe the kind of noise one has to put _ _ _ _ _ _ _ _ _ _ near an airport.

k. I couldn't live _ _ _ _ _ my trustworthy assistant.

l. Dave's lived here _ _ _ _ _ 1998.

m. The kids are _ _ _ _ _ school, and my wife's out shopping.

n. We're going _ _ _ _ _ the cinema - would you like to join us?

o. The article was _ _ _ _ _ the farmers of Peru.

he / to live

a. einfache Gegenwart: _____
b. Verlaufsform der Gegenwart: _____
c. einfache Vergangenheit: _____
d. Vergangenheit mit „used to": _____
e. Verlaufsform der Vergangenheit: _____
f. present perfect: _____
g. Verlaufsform des present perfect: _____
h. Plusquamperfekt: _____
i. Verlaufsform des Plusquamperfekts: _____
j. Zukunft mit „will": _____
k. Zukunft mit „going to": _____
l. future perfect: _____
m. Verlaufsform des future perfect: _____

Lösung 47: a. since b. after c. while d. after/when e. before f. since g. when/after h. before i. while j. until k. until l. while m. when n. until o. since

Lösung 46: a. he lives b. he is living c. he lived d. he used to live e. he was living f. he has lived g. he has been living h. he had lived i. he had been living j. he will live k. he is going to live l. he will have lived m. he will have been living

47. CONJUNCTIONS Setzen Sie die richtigen Konjunktionen ein!

a. Wolfgang has been doing very well _ _ _ _ _ _ _ _ he opened the store.

b. _ _ _ _ _ _ _ _ I had smoked my cigar I enjoyed a glass of brandy.

c. Paul looks after the baby _ _ _ _ _ _ _ _ Janet is playing tennis.

d. The lads went on to a disco _ _ _ _ _ _ _ _ they had finished drinking.

e. I parked the car _ _ _ _ _ _ _ _ we went into the hospital.

f. _ _ _ _ _ _ _ _ my father died we haven't been able to pay our bills.

g. Kathleen took up a position as a nanny _ _ _ _ _ _ _ _ she left school.

h. The national anthem is usually played _ _ _ _ _ _ _ _ the cup final begins.

i. Tim worked at his computer _ _ _ _ _ _ _ _ the children were watching T.V.

j. _ _ _ _ _ _ _ _ he had finished his English essay George was very grumpy.

k. The hooligans continued fighting _ _ _ _ _ _ _ _ the police came.

l. _ _ _ _ _ _ _ _ the plane was landing we kept our seat belts on.

m. _ _ _ _ _ _ _ _ the show was over we went home.

n. We watched a film _ _ _ _ _ _ _ _ it was time to go to bed.

o. _ _ _ _ _ _ _ _ I have started doing these exercises I feel much better.

48. FILL IN THE BLANK Geben Sie die Verbformen an!

a. Have you read that famous book by Nathaniel Hawthorne?
   _ _ _ _ _ it right now.

b. I usually _ _ _ _ _ the bus to work, but yesterday
   I _ _ _ _ _ my bicycle.

c. I _ _ _ _ _ five miles each day.

d. Nigel _ _ _ _ _ to Germany four years ago, and he
   _ _ _ _ _ back to England since then.

e. Will you be there tomorrow? No, I'm afraid I _ _ _ _ _ there.

f. _ _ _ _ _ (you/speak) French? Not really. I _ _ _ _ _ French
   in school, but I _ _ _ _ _ it in ten years.

g. What _ _ _ _ _ when it started to rain?
   I was sailing down the Thames.

h. When you _ _ _ _ _ I was just having a bath.

I/read
take
ride
run
go
not come
not be
you/speak; learned
not speak
you do
call

Lösung 49: a. during/before b. to c. before d. before e. in f. in g. at h. in i. on. j. before k. at l. on m. in n. on o. on

49. IN, AT, ON, TO, DURING, BEFORE Setzen Sie die richtige Präposition ein!

a. _ _ _ _ the war many houses were destroyed.

b. It's a quarter _ _ _ _ ten.

c. Tom's train is late. He won't be here _ _ _ _ eleven.

d. _ _ _ _ his recruitment into the army my uncle was a teacher.

e. When I got up _ _ _ _ the morning I felt unwell.

f. Queen Victoria died _ _ _ _ 1901.

g. We all go to church _ _ _ _ Easter.

h. He got there just _ _ _ _ time.

i. _ _ _ _ Easter Sunday my mother has a lot to do.

j. We left _ _ _ _ the end of the party because I was tired.

k. Harry got to London _ _ _ _ 5 o'clock.

l. He died _ _ _ _ a freezing March day.

m. That was _ _ _ _ the year 1897.

n. Can I have a day off _ _ _ _ Monday?

o. I like reading good books _ _ _ _ the long winter evenings.

50. COMPLETE THE SENTENCES Übersetzen Sie die deutschen Begriffe!

a. This restaurant seems _ _ _ _ _ _ _.   **teuer**

b. But I feel _ _ _ _ _ _ _.   **hungrig**

c. The music sounds _ _ _ _ _ _ _.   **schrecklich**

d. The food smells _ _ _ _ _ _ _.   **köstlich**

e. The bread they bake tastes _ _ _ _ _ _ _.   **ausgezeichnet**

f. But most tables have remained _ _ _ _ _ _ _ so far.   **leer**

g. The waiters look _ _ _ _ _ _ _.   **gelangweilt**

h. My mother will get very _ _ _ _ _ _ _ if we're late.   **ärgerlich**

i. Louise has been feeling _ _ _ _ _ _ _ since Friday.   **krank**

j. She turned _ _ _ _ _ _ _ yesterday at work.   **blass**

k. She told the doctor that she gets _ _ _ _ _ _ _ every time she gets up.   **schwindelig**

l. He has become more _ _ _ _ _ _ _ since his mother started working.   **hilfsbereit**

m. He has lots of _ _ _ _ _ _ _ ideas.   **verrückt**

n. Jim turned out to be _ _ _ _ _ _ _ in his new job.   **erfolgreich**

o. Brian has grown much _ _ _ _ _ _ _ this summer.   **größer**

Lösung 51: a. will be repaired b. was painted c. was put d. was drunk e. will be held
f. is being eaten g. had been hit h. was felt i. will be seen j. has been stolen k. was written
l. be won m. spelled n. spoken o. hung

51. TENSES Wählen Sie die richtige Form aus!

a. The car **will repaired/will be repaired** by us.
b. The building **was painted/was paint** yesterday.
c. The painting **was been putting/was put** on display.
d. A lot of champagne **was drunk/was drunken** at the party.
e. The next Olympic Games **will be held/will be hold** soon.
f. The chocolate **is being eaten/is being ate** by my daughter.
g. She **had been hitted/had been hit** by a tennis ball.
h. The earthquake **was feel/was felt** by everyone in the city.
i. The Queen **will be seen/will see** by many people.
j. The money **has been stole/has been stolen** by a robber.
k. Macbeth **was written/was wrote** by Shakespeare.
l. The race will probably **be win/be won** by an African runner.
m. How is this word **spelled/spelt**?
n. The little girl **was spoke/spoken** to by her teacher.
o. The wet clothes **were hung/hanged** from a clothesline.

52. PASSIVE Verwandeln Sie die folgenden Sätze ins Passiv!

a. Tom will supply drinks for the party.
b. I sent the watch back to the shop.
c. They have built a new hotel.
d. The boy eats an apple every day.
e. I lost the key to the back door.
f. They play football at my school.
g. The dog was chasing a rabbit.
h. Tom takes photos every day.
i. The professor is correcting our papers.
j. Many boys enjoy sport.
k. We were mowing the lawn.
l. They gave her a watch.
m. We feed the ducks in the evening.
n. A bee stung her.
o. A storm flooded the roads.

a. Drinks _____
b. The watch _____
c. A new hotel _____
d. An apple _____
e. The key _____
f. Football _____
g. A rabbit _____
h. Photos _____
i. Our papers _____
j. Sport _____
k. The lawn _____
l. A watch _____
m. The ducks _____
n. She _____
o. The roads _____

Lösung 53: a. arose; arisen b. froze; frozen c. acted; acted d. lent; lent e. watched; watched
f. unwound; unwound g. split; split h. reset; reset i. drank; drunk j. swam; swum
k. strode; stridden l. tried; tried m. attempted; attempted n. drew; drawn o. wrote; written

Lösung 52: a. will be supplied b. was sent c. has been built d. is eaten e. was lost f. is played
g. was being chased h. are taken i. are being corrected j. is enjoyed k. was being mowed/mown
l. was given m. are fed n. was stung o. were flooded

53. PAST TENSE Geben Sie die Vergangenheitsformen an!

a. arise,

b. freeze,

c. act,

d. lend,

e. watch,

f. unwind,

g. split,

h. reset,

i. drink,

j. swim,

k. stride,

l. try,

m. attempt,

n. draw,

o. write,

a. You may not go out _ _ _ _ _ you have finished your homework.

b. Claudia opened the door _ _ _ _ _ it was too hot inside.

c. The nurse gave the man the kiss of life _ _ _ _ _ she wanted to save him.

d. Sarah took her umbrella _ _ _ _ _ it was raining.

e. My mother wasn't sure _ _ _ _ _ I would be home in time for dinner.

f. _ _ _ _ _ he is unemployed he always seems happy.

g. _ _ _ _ _ you study hard you will pass your exams.

h. The match will not restart _ _ _ _ _ the spectators stop fighting.

i. She spent a year in Ireland _ _ _ _ _ she wanted to improve her English.

j. Lola wanted to go to university _ _ _ _ _ her father couldn't afford it.

k. Times were so hard _ _ _ _ _ Frank couldn't even get a holiday job.

l. Debbie works hard _ _ _ _ _ she is not bright enough to do this course.

m. I will buy you a new motorbike _ _ _ _ _ you pass your exams.

n. We do our homework early _ _ _ _ _ we like to watch TV at night.

o. Please give me a ring _ _ _ _ _ you can't come to the party.

Lösung 55: a. rains b. raining c. writes d. are damaging; lands e. is playing f. lives; is staying g. is waiting h. don't believe i. is working j. do k. take l. wants m. is smoking n. are taking o. receives

Lösung 54: a. until b. because c. because d. as/because e. if/whether f. Although g. If
h. until i. because j. but k. that l. but m. if/when n. because o. if

55. SIMPLE PRESENT OR PRESENT CONTINUOUS? Setzen Sie die richtige Verbform ein!

a. It frequently _ _ _ _ _ _ in Ireland. — **rain**

b. Is it _ _ _ _ _ _ there now? — **rain**

c. Susan _ _ _ _ _ _ to her parents every Sunday night. — **write**

d. You _ _ _ _ _ the flowers every time the ball _ _ _ _ _ in the flower beds. — **damage/land**

e. Where is Kevin? He _ _ _ _ _ _ squash with Sue. — **play**

f. Normally she _ _ _ _ in Northbridge but she _ _ _ _ with friends at present. — **live/stay**

g. Hurry up, the examiner _ _ _ _ _ _ to begin. — **wait**

h. I _ _ _ _ _ _ _ _ _ _ _ _ a word Timothy says. — **not/believe**

i. The new lawnmower _ _ _ _ _ _ very well at the moment. — **work**

j. What _ _ _ _ _ _ you do for a living? — **do**

k. As a secretary I _ _ _ _ _ _ hundreds of letters a week. — **take**

l. My boss _ _ _ _ _ _ to change jobs soon. — **want**

m. Look! She _ _ _ _ _ _ in the non-smoking zone again. — **smoke**

n. We _ _ _ _ _ _ our break now, Mr. Smith. — **take**

o. The tennis star _ _ _ _ _ _ a lot of fan mail. — **receive**

a. _ _ _ _ _ Pat or Walter will put in the advertisement for you.

b. _ _ _ _ _ of the candidates will be interviewed at length.

c. I read the newspaper _ _ _ _ _ day of the week.

d. _ _ _ _ _ time I was in Ireland it was raining.

e. _ _ _ _ _ of the children caught a bad cold this winter.

f. You mean you have _ _ _ _ _ money in your purse?

g. _ _ _ _ _ dress will do. It's only a casual party.

h. Jim visited us _ _ _ _ _ morning last week.

i. Have you got _ _ _ _ _ idea when he's coming home?

j. _ _ _ _ _ I'm going crazy or it's snowing in the month of June.

k. _ _ _ _ _ could do the puzzle.

l. Take _ _ _ _ _ the red or the blue dress.

m. Have you _ _ _ _ _ milk?

n. I'm afraid we have _ _ _ _ _ left.

o. Chris threw a party but _ _ _ _ _ came.

Lösung 57: a. had b. above c. were drinking d. for e. went f. eat g. have never been
h. a sore throat i. fast j. wrote k. think l. a day m. swimming n. drove o. is shining

Lösung 56: a. either b. each c. every d. every/each e. each f. no g. any h. every/each
i. any j. either k. nobody/anybody l. either m. any n. none o. nobody

57. FILL IN THE BLANK Welches Wort gehört in die Lücke?

a. They noticed that they _ _ _ _ _ _ (have/had) forgotten their money.

b. The painting is _ _ _ _ _ _ (above/up) the fireplace.

c. At four o'clock, they _ _ _ _ _ _ (were drinking/are drinking) coffee.

d. Jennifer has been here _ _ _ _ _ _ (since/for) three weeks.

e. Yesterday I _ _ _ _ _ _ (go/went) home.

f. When he was small, Robert used to _ _ _ _ _ _ (eat/be eating) chocolate.

g. I _ _ _ _ _ _ (never was/have never been) to Scotland.

h. I've got _ _ _ _ _ _ (a sore throat/a throat ache) today.

i. She runs very _ _ _ _ _ _. (fastly/fast)

j. This morning I _ _ _ _ _ _ (wrote/have written) a little poem.

k. What do you _ _ _ _ _ _ (thinking/think) about this?

l. Most people brush their teeth twice _ _ _ _ _ _ (on a day/a day).

m. He's good at _ _ _ _ _ _ (swimming/to swim).

n. Yesterday, Gerald _ _ _ _ _ _ (has driven/drove) to Edinburgh.

o. At the moment, the sun _ _ _ _ _ _. (shines/is shining)

58. INFINITIVE OR "ING-FORM"? Setzen Sie die richtige Verbform ein!

a. By _ _ _ _ _ _ the crocodile he made the swimming pool safe.

b. He left the house without _ _ _ _ _ _ goodbye.

c. _ _ _ _ _ _ on the beach is very relaxing.

d. At first I enjoyed _ _ _ _ _ _ to him.

e. But after a while I got tired _ _ _ _ _ _ his complaints.

f. I would not want _ _ _ _ _ _ like him.

g. It's not much use _ _ _ _ _ _ a bike if you don't ride it.

h. I've always enjoyed _ _ _ _ _ _ - it's healthy and relaxing.

i. I'm really tired and I'd like _ _ _ _ _ _ some rest.

j. The boss wanted Hopkins _ _ _ _ _ _ the report by 9 a.m.

k. Our employer doesn't allow _ _ _ _ _ _ on the job.

l. How about _ _ _ _ _ _ me next week?

m. We didn't want to risk _ _ _ _ _ _ injured.

n. Try to hammer in that nail without _ _ _ _ _ _ your thumb, OK?

o. Tanya denied _ _ _ _ _ _ the watch.

to kill
to say
to lie
to listen
to hear
to be
to have
to swim
to get
to finish
to smoke
to visit
to be
to hit
to steal

Lösung 59: a. we eat b. we are eating c. we ate d. we used to eat e. we were eating f. we have eaten g. we have been eating h. we had eaten i. we had been eating j. we will eat k. we are going to eat l. we will have eaten m. we will have been eating

59. A TENSE MOMENT Geben Sie die richtigen Formen des Verbs an!

we / to eat

a. *einfache Gegenwart:*

b. *Verlaufsform der Gegenwart:*

c. *einfache Vergangenheit:*

d. *Vergangenheit mit used to:*

e. *Verlaufsform der Vergangenheit:*

f. *present perfect:*

g. *Verlaufsform des present perfect:*

h. *Plusquamperfekt:*

i. *Verlaufsform des Plusquamperfekts:*

j. *Zukunft mit will:*

k. *Zukunft mit going to:*

l. *future perfect:*

m. *Verlaufsform des future perfect:*

60. GET ON WITH IT Setzen Sie die richtige Präposition ein!

a. Jane saw the knife _ _ _ _ the table.

b. The post office is _ _ _ _ O'Connell Street.

c. She was waiting _ _ _ _ the door when we got home.

d. The money fell _ _ _ _ his shirt pocket.

e. Mary got _ _ _ _ the car and drove away.

f. She has just come _ _ _ _ London.

g. Peter got _ _ _ _ the bus and walked _ _ _ _ the bank.

h. The boy standing _ _ _ _ the left-hand side _ _ _ _ the road whistled.

i. The girls _ _ _ _ work are always laughing _ _ _ _ Jane.

j. I grew up _ _ _ _ a farm.

k. We met _ _ _ _ the school where I was teaching.

l. Could you collect Patrick _ _ _ _ the train station?

m. Did you enjoy yourself _ _ _ _ the party?

n. We went _ _ _ _ the cinema and sat down.

o. Tom took _ _ _ _ a bag of chips and offered us some.

about

in

at

on

to

into

out (of)

from

off

around

towards

Lösung 61: a. harder; hardest b. more/most probably c. better; best d. sooner; soonest
e. more/most quietly f. more/most animatedly g. more/most sarcastically h. more/most noisily
i. more; most j. more/most noticeably k. more/most slyly l. more/most completely
m. more/most gracefully n. more/most alertly o. more/most easily

61. HARD, HARDER, HARDEST Bilden Sie die Steigerungsformen!

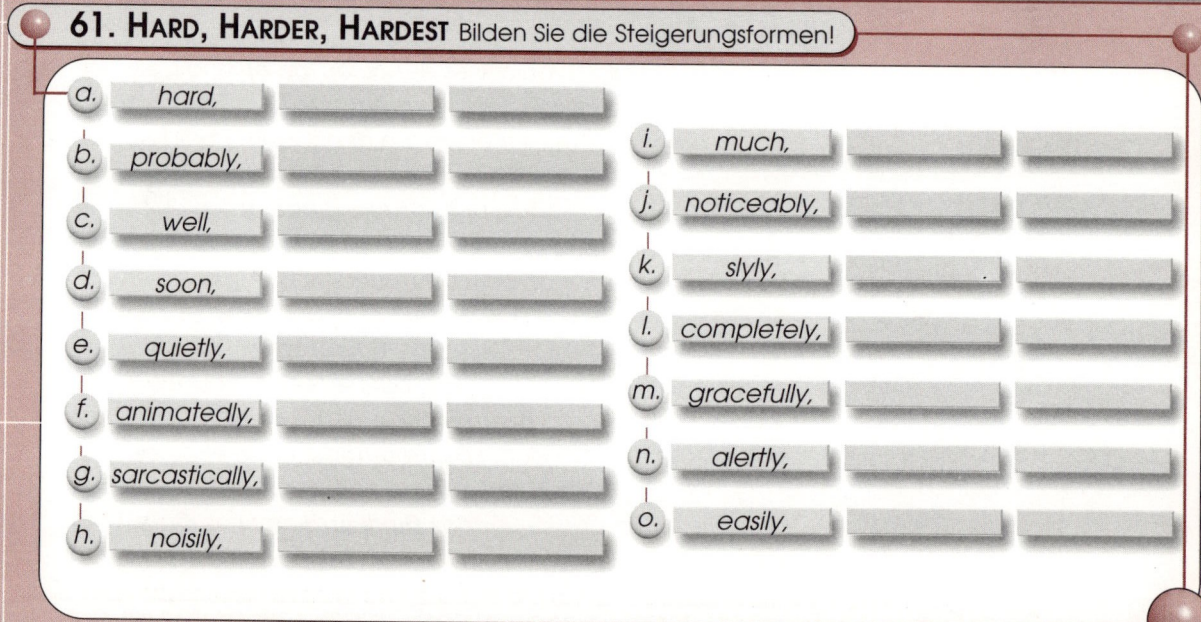

a. hard,

b. probably,

c. well,

d. soon,

e. quietly,

f. animatedly,

g. sarcastically,

h. noisily,

i. much,

j. noticeably,

k. slyly,

l. completely,

m. gracefully,

n. alertly,

o. easily,

62. INFINITIVE OR PRESENT CONTINUOUS Kreisen Sie die richtige Form ein!

a. I enjoy **to eat/eating** .
b. We agree **to help/helping** you.
c. He is prepared **to take part/taking** part.
d. She gave up **to learn/learning** French.
e. They have finished **to work/working**.
f. I'll arrange **to see/seeing** him.
g. She seems **to be/being** happy.
h. They're regretting **to leave/leaving** London.
i. Please practise **to touch/touching** your toes.
j. She prevented her little sister from **to hurt/hurting** herself.
k. It's no use **to complain/complaining**!
l. I want him **to come/coming** along.
m. We didn't manage **to do/doing** the housework.
n. appreciate **to learn/learning** the piano.
o. She's busy **to do/doing** the shopping.

Lösung 63: a. hasn't given b. is; leaves; will be c. Are you going to visit; visited d. met e. has been f. prefer g. are h. ate i. won't be j. are; will show

63. FILL IN THE BLANK Geben Sie die Verbformen an!

a. Our waiter _ _ _ _ _ us our menus yet. — **not give**

b. There _ _ _ _ a train to Brighton that _ _ _ _ at 10 o'clock on Sunday. — **be; leave**
I can't take that train. On Sunday I _ _ _ _ _ busy at 10 o'clock. — **be**

c. _ _ _ _ _ us again tomorrow? Yes, even though I _ _ _ _ _ you yesterday as well. — **you/visit; visit**

d. I had never met Brian's wife Liz, but I _ _ _ _ _ her yesterday. — **meet**

e. Basketball _ _ _ _ _ my favourite sport for the last ten years. — **be**

f. I used to prefer watching basketball, but now I _ _ _ _ _ watching football. — **prefer**

g. Today there _ _ _ _ _ no meetings. — **be**

h. Last week she _ _ _ _ _ scrambled eggs for the first time. — **eat**

i. I will be somewhere else tomorrow. I _ _ _ _ _ here. — **not be**

j. I know that you _ _ _ _ a stranger in London. So I _ _ _ _ you around. — **be; show**

64. PASSIVE Verwandeln Sie die folgenden Sätze ins Passiv!

a. The doctors have taken her to the hospital.
b. The judge will pass judgement tomorrow.
c. She hits the child too often.
d. Lightning struck the house.
e. We have invited Jane.
f. They cancelled the meeting.
g. They have changed the date.
h. They have included overtime in the bill.
i. Parents should send children to good schools.
j. Someone had turned the oven on.
k. We will hold the party at my house.
l. Her friends presented her with some flowers.
m. The tailor made some adjustments to my suit.
n. His daughter gave me a kiss on the cheek.
o. Terry missed the bus.

a. She _____
b. Judgement _____
c. The child _____
d. The house _____
e. Jane _____
f. The meeting _____
g. The date _____
h. Overtime _____
i. Children _____
j. The oven _____
k. The party _____
l. Some flowers _____
m. Some adjustments _____
n. A kiss on the cheek _____
o. The bus _____

Lösung 65: a. loves b. is touring c. asks d. am taking e. gives f. makes g. goes h. is departing i. are having j. are you baking k. don't sell l. takes m. am wearing n. belong o. is leaking

Lösung 64: a. has been taken b. will be passed c. is hit d. was struck e. has been invited
f. was cancelled g. has been changed h. has been included i. should be sent
j. had been turned on k. will be held l. were presented m. were made n. was given
o. was missed

65. SIMPLE PRESENT OR PRESENT CONTINUOUS? Setzen Sie die richtige Verbform ein!

a.	Dorothy _ _ _ _ _ to read a good novel on holiday.	love
b.	My brother _ _ _ _ _ Italy even as I speak.	tour
c.	Tom _ _ _ _ _ the strangest questions in class.	ask
d.	Dad, I _ _ _ _ _ ten pounds out of your wallet.	take
e.	My mother _ _ _ _ _ a party for her friends once a year.	give
f.	Such behaviour _ _ _ _ _ me furious.	make
g.	He usually _ _ _ _ _ out on a Saturday night.	go
h.	She _ _ _ _ _ by train from Liverpool today.	depart
i.	They _ _ _ _ _ a game of cards now.	have
j.	What you _ _ _ _ _, Mom?	bake
k.	Songs which are not popular_ _ _ _ _ very well.	not/sell
l.	A drug addict _ _ _ _ _ drugs.	take
m.	I _ _ _ _ _ a hat today because it's a special occasion.	wear
n.	Do you _ _ _ _ _ to the club?	belong
o.	The car _ _ _ _ _ oil. Can you fix it?	leak

66. NUMBERS Schreiben Sie die Zahlen in Buchstaben aus!

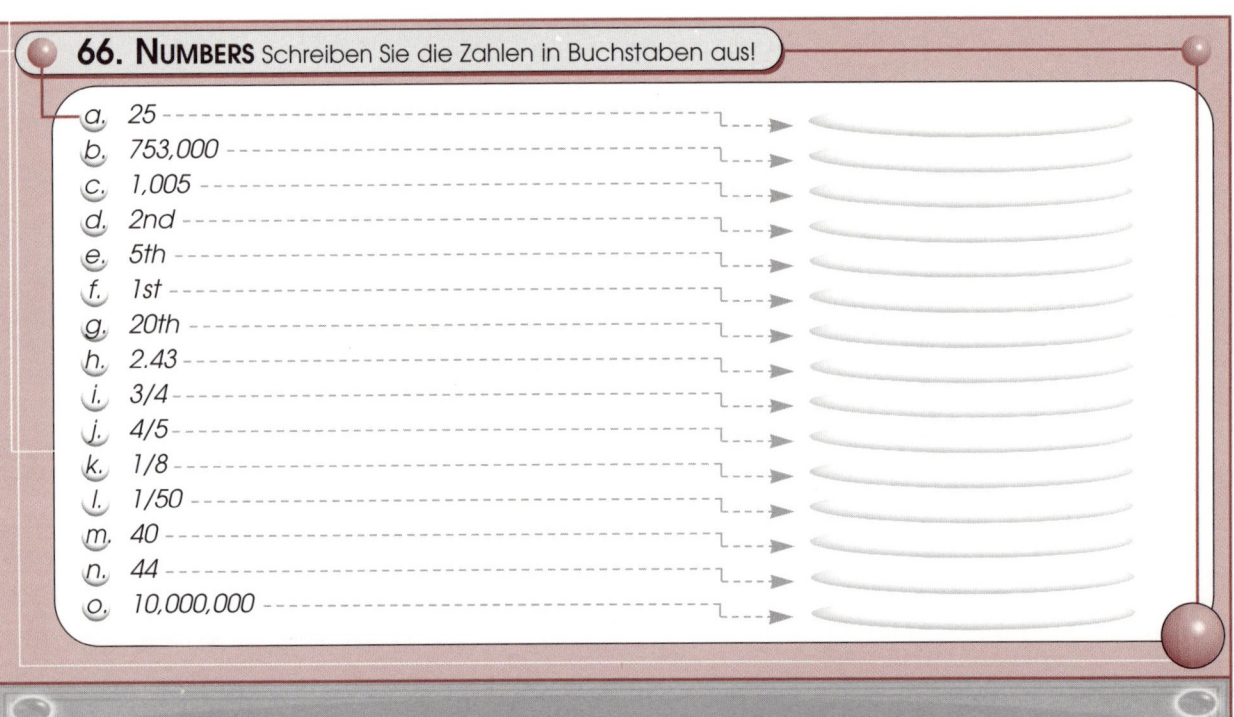

a. 25 --- ⟶

b. 753,000 ----------------------------------- ⟶

c. 1,005 --------------------------------------- ⟶

d. 2nd -- ⟶

e. 5th --- ⟶

f. 1st -- ⟶

g. 20th --------------------------------------- ⟶

h. 2.43 -- ⟶

i. 3/4 --- ⟶

j. 4/5 --- ⟶

k. 1/8 --- ⟶

l. 1/50 -- ⟶

m. 40 --- ⟶

n. 44 -- ⟶

o. 10,000,000 ------------------------------- ⟶

Lösung 67: a. arrived; saw b. are you doing; I'm looking; seen c. will see; will be coming
d. haven't reserved e. rises f. realized; had g. be; isn't h. bought; had walked; realized; didn't fit

67. FILL IN THE BLANK Geben Sie die Verbformen an!

a. Yesterday I _ _ _ _ _ _ at the station, and I was expecting to see Liz, but instead I _ _ _ _ _ _ Sarah. — *arrive* / *see*

b. What _ _ _ _ _ _ at the moment? _ _ _ _ _ _ for a trolley. Have you _ _ _ _ _ _ one? — *you/do; I/look* / *see*

c. I _ _ _ _ _ _ Jason tomorrow - he _ _ _ _ _ _ to visit me. — *see; come*

d. I _ _ _ _ _ _ a hotel room yet. — *not reserve*

e. The sun _ _ _ _ _ _ in the east every morning. — *rise*

f. I had already ordered a steak when I _ _ _ _ _ _ that I _ _ _ _ _ _ no money. — *realize* / *have*

g. That hotel always used to _ _ _ _ _ _ very expensive, but now it _ _ _ _ _ _ very expensive. — *be* / *not be*

h. Yesterday I _ _ _ _ _ _ a pair of shoes at the shoe shop. After I _ _ _ _ _ _ about a hundred yards I _ _ _ _ _ _ that the shoes _ _ _ _ _ _. — *buy* / *walk; realize* / *not fit*

68. MUST/MUSTN'T, HAVE TO/DON'T HAVE TO, NEED/NEEDN'T Setzen Sie diese Formen ein!

a. Derek has been drinking all day. He _ _ _ _ _ be drunk.

b. Anna is much smaller than you are. You _ _ _ _ _ hit her.

c. Sara _ _ _ _ _ practise more often if she wants to be good at chess.

d. I _ _ _ _ _ leave now. My mother is expecting me.

e. You _ _ _ _ _ come home at Christmas but your mother would love it if you did.

f. I've got an appointment so I _ _ _ _ _ leave now.

g. "John and Sue - getting married?" "You _ _ _ _ _ be joking!"

h. We _ _ _ _ _ forget to lock the door before we leave.

i. Financially I _ _ _ _ _ work as my wife is rich, but I like working anyway.

j. It was absolutely free; we _ _ _ _ _ pay a penny.

k. Alan travels to America each week. That _ _ _ _ _ be very tiring.

l. If you want to get there by five you _ _ _ _ _ take a taxi.

m. Good little boys and girls _ _ _ _ _ do as they are told.

n. If you want to join the army, you _ _ _ _ _ pass a physical examination.

o. You _ _ _ _ _ touch that! It's scalding hot!

Lösung 69: a. has lived b. have you studied c. has been d. swim e. is learning
f. have been serving g. have smoked h. need i. drive j. spoke k. have tried l. has worn
m. asked n. have waited o. has lived

69. VERB TENSES Wählen Sie die richtige Verbform aus!

a. He **is living/has lived** in London for 20 years.
b. How long **do you study/have you studied** here?
c. She **is/has been** here for 2 years.
d. I **swim/have swum** every morning.
e. She **is learning/has learned** English at the moment.
f. We **are/have been serving** customers since 1955.
g. I **smoke/have smoked** cigarettes since I was 19.
h. I **need/have needed** a cup of coffee to wake up in the morning.
i. I **drive/have driven** a bus, and I always have.
j. I **spoke/have spoken** to him every day from 1995 to 1997.
k. I **try/have tried**, but it has never worked.
l. He **wore/has worn** a tie before, but not recently.
m. He **asked/has asked** politely, but I still said no.
n. I **wait/have waited** for over an hour.
o. Lee **lives/has lived** here for years.

70. -SELF, -SELVES, EACH OTHER, ONE ANOTHER Was muss in der Lücke stehen?

a. Diane went to the station to buy _ _ _ _ _ a ticket.
b. Perry and Fred can't stand being in _ _ _ _ _ company.
c. This do-it-_ _ _ _ _ book is far too complicated.
d. George wrote the song _ _ _ _ _ as a present for Mary.
e. This letter is to be given to Alan _ _ _ _ _ and not his secretary or anyone else.
f. Lads, help _ _ _ _ _ to some food.
g. Denise doesn't know _ _ _ _ _ since she got a new haircut.
h. John and Kathleen gave _ _ _ _ _ presents for Christmas.
i. They help _ _ _ _ _ as much as they can.
j. I like to read _ _ _ _ _ to sleep.
k. Jack bought _ _ _ _ _ a computer for his birthday.
l. So you're off to Wales! We're going to York _ _ _ _ _.
m. I'm kicking _ _ _ _ _ for missing my big chance.
n. Give _ _ _ _ _ a kiss and make up.
o. If you're innocent you should turn _ _ _ _ _ in and face the courts.

Lösung 71: a. Tom usually goes b. korrekt c. get up early d. korrekt e. korrekt f. hardly worth g. korrekt h. korrekt i. spoke nicely j. gazed lovingly k. Scarcely had the Indians/The Indians had scarcely l. korrekt m. a mile daily n. korrekt o. to dress casually

71. NOT QUITE RIGHT Haben die unterstrichenen Adverbien die richtige Position?

a. Tom goes _usually_ to the bank on Friday.
b. He went to the hospital as _fast_ as he could.
c. The Smiths had to _early_ get up the day they travelled to India.
d. He _jokingly_ threw the ball out the window.
e. It landed _exactly_ on Mr. Fenton's new lorry.
f. _Hardly_ it's worth mentioning.
g. _Furiously_ grabbing his umbrella, he marched out the door.
h. The opera singer performed very _well_.
i. Alan _nicely_ spoke to the woman who had lost her purse.
j. _Lovingly_ she gazed across the room at her boyfriend.
k. _Scarcely_ the Indians had seen the cowboys when they fled.
l. The cowboys _bravely_ fought them off.
m. Jim _daily_ jogs a mile.
n. Turtles tend to move _slowly_.
o. Employees are _casually_ not encouraged to dress.

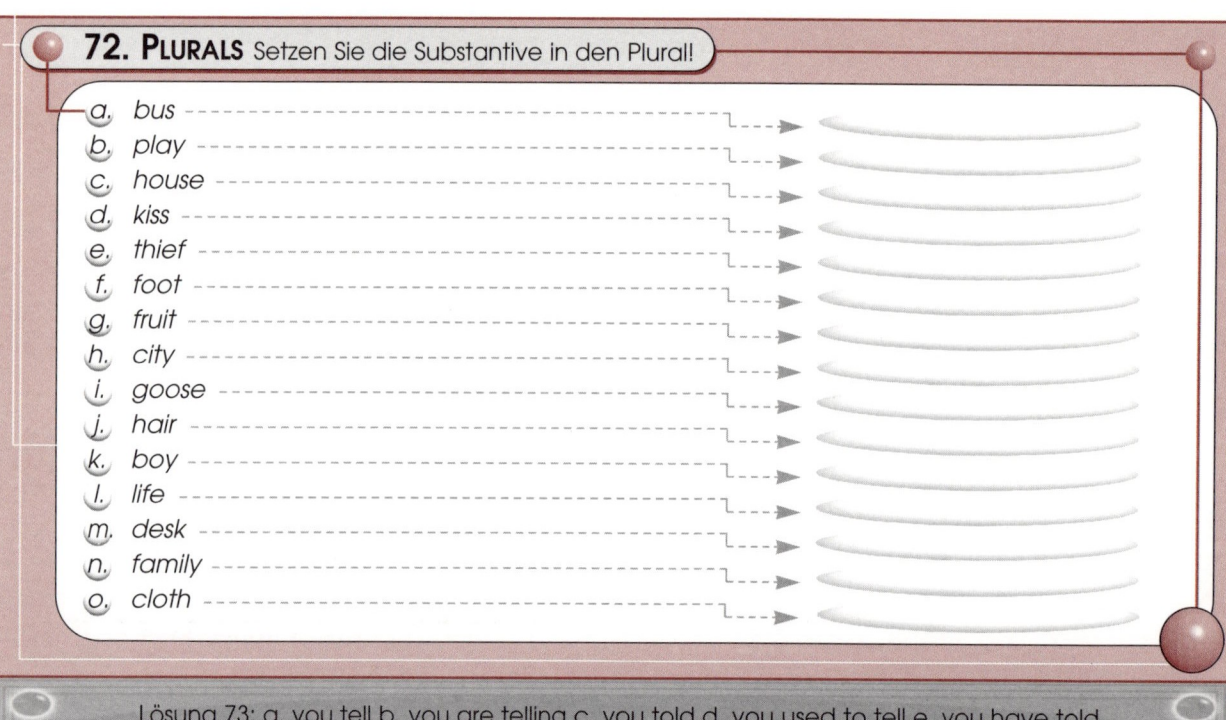

72. PLURALS Setzen Sie die Substantive in den Plural!

a. bus --- ➤
b. play -- ➤
c. house --------------------------------------- ➤
d. kiss -- ➤
e. thief --------------------------------------- ➤
f. foot -- ➤
g. fruit --------------------------------------- ➤
h. city -- ➤
i. goose --------------------------------------- ➤
j. hair -- ➤
k. boy --- ➤
l. life -- ➤
m. desk -- ➤
n. family -------------------------------------- ➤
o. cloth --------------------------------------- ➤

Lösung 73: a. you tell b. you are telling c. you told d. you used to tell e. you have told
f. you were telling g. you have been telling h. you had told i. you had been telling
j. you are going to tell k. you will tell

73. TENSES Geben Sie die richtigen Formen des Verbs an!

you / to tell

a. *einfache Gegenwart:* _____

b. *Verlaufsform der Gegenwart:* _____

c. *einfache Vergangenheit:* _____

d. *Vergangenheit mit „used to":* _____

e. *Verlaufsform der Vergangenheit:* _____

f. *present perfect:* _____

g. *Verlaufsform des present perfect:* _____

h. *Plusquamperfekt:* _____

i. *Verlaufsform des Plusquamperfekts:* _____

j. *Zukunft mit „will":* _____

k. *Zukunft mit „going to":* _____

l. *future perfect:* _____

m. *Verlaufsform des future perfect:* _____

a. I'd like to talk to you about _ _ _ history.

b. What history do I mean? _ _ _ history of _ _ _ art or _ _ _ history of _ _ _ science?

c. Well, I'm especially interested in _ _ _ history of _ _ _ old sailing ships.

d. Just think of _ _ _ voyage Christopher Columbus and his sailors made in 1492!

e. _ _ _ courage was needed to take part in such a journey.

f. _ _ _ courage the sailors had to show in storms for example was great.

g. Surely they were afraid of _ _ _ death.

h. But what do you think _ _ _ main problem was?

i. Was it _ _ _ time these voyages took?

j. Perhaps, yes, but it is also possible that _ _ _ morale was the biggest problem.

k. And it was not easy to provide _ _ _ water fifty sailors and the passengers needed.

l. _ _ _ death of passengers was very often caused by bad food.

m. As _ _ _ sailors had to work very hard, they needed good food.

n. " _ _ _ life is always harder than you wish it were", you might say.

o. I researched the article with _ _ _ help of a friend.

75. WHAT'S WRONG? Finden Sie den Fehler im Satz!

a. I get up always at 5 a.m.
b. Bobby disliked to do that.
c. I call you tomorrow.
d. My stomach hurt because I had ate too much.
e. It's autumn, and the leafs are falling.
f. The love is a wonderful thing.
g. Remember me if I forget, will you?
h. I yesterday realized what I've been doing wrong.
i. Fred refused himself to try it.
j. My sisters offered they're help, but I refused.
k. I hitted the bully when he insulted me.
l. The more I hear, the suspiciouser I get.
m. And last not least, my cousins Terry and Jerry.
n. I learn English since I moved to Brisbane.
o. My glasses is broken - I need to buy another one.

76. FILL IN THE BLANK Setzen Sie die richtige Form ein!

a. I prefer _ _ _ _ _ _ to see my friends. — **to go**

b. He likes to practise _ _ _ _ _ _ guitar. — **to play**

c. Tim enjoys _ _ _ _ _ _ to France. — **to travel**

d. I want you to stop _ _ _ _ _ _ about it. — **to talk**

e. I'm finished _ _ _ _ _ _ this book. — **to read**

f. Does your hair need _ _ _ _ _ _? — **to cut**

g. The room needs _ _ _ _ _ _. — **to clean**

h. Tony suggests _ _ _ _ _ _ out to a restaurant. — **to go**

i. They are talking about _ _ _ _ _ _ a holiday. — **to take**

j. I'm looking forward to _ _ _ _ _ _ my girlfriend. — **to see**

k. Jason is not good at _ _ _ _ _ _ presents. — **to buy**

l. There's no use in _ _ _ _ _ _ there every day. — **to go**

m. _ _ _ _ _ _ in the rain is no fun. — **to walk**

n. I can't help _ _ _ _ _ _. — **to cry**

o. I'm going to try _ _ _ _ _ _ a garden this spring. — **to plant**

Lösung 77: a. and b. or c. because d. when/as e. as soon as f. because g. as h. in case i. as/when j. that k. as long as l. whenever m. both ... and n. neither ... nor o. until

77. CONJUNCTIONS Setzen Sie die passenden Konjunktionen ein!

a. Alice is going to go to Sicily for a week _ _ _ _ _ _ Martin isn't.

b. Would you like red wine _ _ _ _ _ _ do you prefer white?

c. John was happy _ _ _ _ _ _ he got promoted.

d. The car started _ _ _ _ _ _ she turned the key.

e. _ _ _ _ _ _ I start up the barbecue, it always begins to rain.

f. He turned down the offer _ _ _ _ _ _ it didn't sound good.

g. He belted out the song _ _ _ _ _ _ only he could.

h. He always took an umbrella with him _ _ _ _ _ _ it should rain.

i. She had tears in her eyes _ _ _ _ _ _ she left the theatre.

j. They were so proud of her _ _ _ _ _ _ they gave a big party.

k. _ _ _ _ _ _ you take it easy, you won't be stressed out.

l. _ _ _ _ _ _ Lorna visits London she goes to the National Gallery.

m. Tom had enough time to visit _ _ _ _ the castle _ _ _ _ the church.

n. _ _ _ _ _ _ Darren _ _ _ _ _ _ Father heard her calling.

o. Mr. Oldridge knew his way _ _ _ _ _ _ it got dark.

| und |
| oder |
| denn |
| als |
| sobald |
| weil |
| wie |
| falls |
| als |
| dass |
| solange |
| jedes Mal, wenn |
| sowohl ... als auch |
| weder ... noch |
| bis |

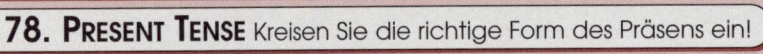

78. PRESENT TENSE Kreisen Sie die richtige Form des Präsens ein!

a. I always **get up/am getting** up at six in the morning.
b. I can **see/seeing** the lake.
c. He **drinks/is drinking** tea at the moment.
d. She **wants/is wanting** to go to the cinema.
e. What **does this word mean/is this word meaning**?
f. What **do you do/are you doing** today?
g. Eric **sees/is seeing** a psychiatrist.
h. I **think/am thinking** about you at the moment.
i. I **have/am having** lunch with her next week.
j. She usually **travels/is travelling** by train.
k. Terri **knows/is knowing** what to do.
l. Wayne **needs/is needing** a new watch.
m. It **rains/It's raining** outside.
n. He **looks/is looking** for a place to stay.
o. He **walks/is walking** the dog at the moment.

Lösung 79: a. skinnier; skinniest b. younger; youngest c. colder; coldest d. taller; tallest
e. fitter; fittest f. more crowded; most crowded g. worse; worst h. more beautiful; most beautiful
i. sharper; sharpest j. paler; palest k. rangier; rangiest l. hotter; hottest m. more pitiful; most
pitiful n. more curious; most curious o. more confident; most confident

79. GOOD, BETTER, BEST Geben Sie Komparativ und Superlativ an!

a. skinny,

b. young,

c. cold,

d. tall,

e. fit,

f. crowded,

g. bad,

h. beautiful,

i. sharp,

j. pale,

k. rangy,

l. hot,

m. pitiful,

n. curious,

o. confident,

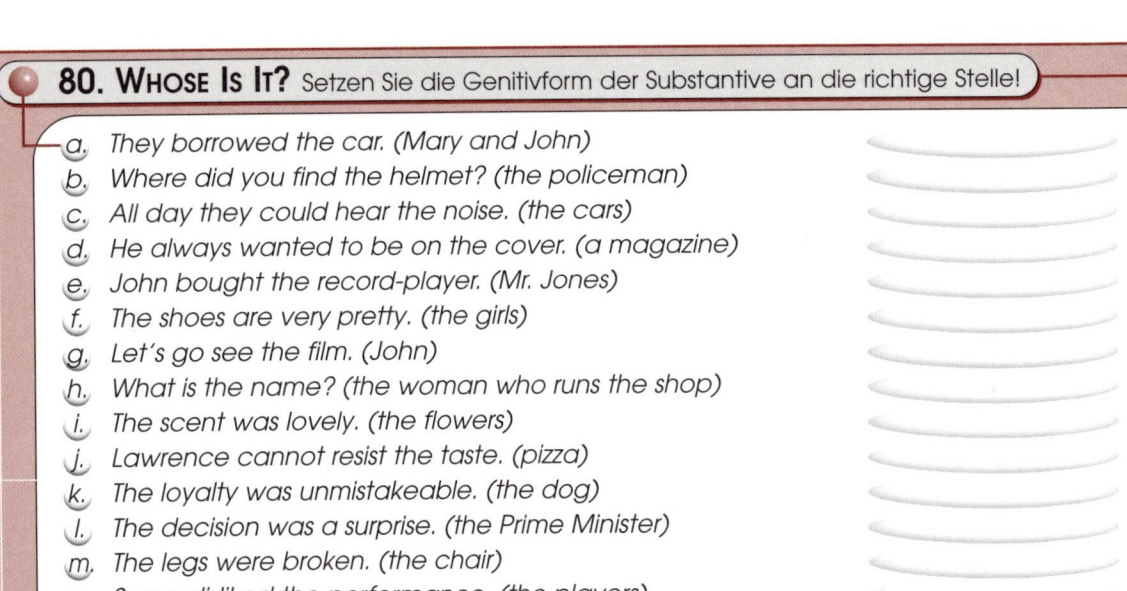

80. WHOSE IS IT? Setzen Sie die Genitivform der Substantive an die richtige Stelle!

a. They borrowed the car. (Mary and John)

b. Where did you find the helmet? (the policeman)

c. All day they could hear the noise. (the cars)

d. He always wanted to be on the cover. (a magazine)

e. John bought the record-player. (Mr. Jones)

f. The shoes are very pretty. (the girls)

g. Let's go see the film. (John)

h. What is the name? (the woman who runs the shop)

i. The scent was lovely. (the flowers)

j. Lawrence cannot resist the taste. (pizza)

k. The loyalty was unmistakeable. (the dog)

l. The decision was a surprise. (the Prime Minister)

m. The legs were broken. (the chair)

n. Some disliked the performance. (the players)

o. The members are very enthusiastic. (choir)

Lösung 81: a. American b. German c. Australian d. Thai e. Italian f. Japanese g. Swiss h. English
i. French j. Scottish k. Spanish l. Welsh m. Chinese n. Portuguese o. Swedish

Lösung 80: a. Mary and John's car b. the policeman's helmet c. the noise of the cars d. on the cover of a magazine e. Mr. Jones'/Mr. Jones's record-player f. The girls' shoes g. John's film h. of the woman who runs i. The scent of the flowers j. the taste of pizza k. The dog's loyalty l. The Prime Minister's decision m. The legs of the chair n. the players' performances o. The members of the choir

81. NATIONALITIES Bilden Sie das prädikative Adjektiv mit „to be"!

a. Tom is from America. Tom is ----------------→

b. Susanne is from Germany. Susanne is ----------→

c. Dan is from Australia. Dan is ----------------→

d. Eugene is from Thailand. Eugene is ----------→

e. Antonella is from Italy. Antonella is ----------→

f. Mariko is from Japan. Mariko is --------------→

g. Bernd is from Switzerland. Bernd is ----------→

h. Gordon is from England. Gordon is ----------→

i. Pierre is from France. Pierre is --------------→

j. Moira is from Scotland. Moira is ------------→

k. Fernando is from Spain. Fernando is ----------→

l. Mary is from Wales. Mary is ----------------→

m. Lee is from China. Lee is ------------------→

n. Sandra is from Portugal. Sandra is ----------→

o. Malin is from Sweden. Malin is ------------→

82. FILL IN THE BLANK Setzen Sie die passende Präposition ein!

a. Let's not let anything come _ _ _ us.
b. David lives _ _ _ a cottage _ _ _ the Post Office.
c. The man sitting _ _ _ Julie was wearing a huge hat.
d. No one wants to live _ _ _ the factory.
e. Philip stood _ _ _ the chair so that he could replace a light-bulb.
f. Andrew put his new painting _ _ _ the wall _ _ _ the fireplace.
g. She finally found the wedding-ring _ _ _ a pile of laundry.
h. Mr. and Mrs. Prentice enjoyed paddling _ _ _ the river in their canoe.
i. The Thorntons always go on holiday _ _ _ Easter.
j. Last night I watched TV _ _ _ 1 a.m..
k. The English Civil War occurred more than 340 years _ _ _.
l. Gladstone could not walk _ _ _ a bookshop without going in.
m. Lucy went _ _ _ Harvard to take her degree.
n. We went _ _ _ the theatre _ _ _ taxi.
o. Joan hasn't had a vacation _ _ _ last summer.

zwischen
in; neben
vor
in der Nähe von
auf
an; über
unter
über
zu
bis
vor
an ... vorbei
nach
in; mit
seit

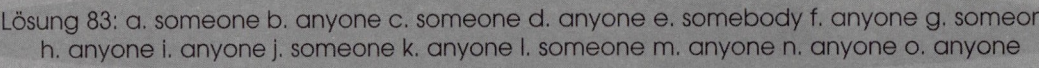

83. SOMEONE OR ANYONE? Entscheiden Sie, was in die Lücke kommt!

a. I'm looking for _ _ _ _ _ _ called Robert Taylor.

b. We don't know _ _ _ _ _ _ named Taylor.

c. Is there _ _ _ _ _ _ who can take me to London?

d. There isn't _ _ _ _ _ _ who is going to London.

e. Does _ _ _ _ _ _ sell fish here?

f. No there isn't _ _ _ _ _ _ in this village who does.

g. Has _ _ _ _ _ _ got a brochure from the hotel?

h. Isn't there _ _ _ _ _ _ who has got a brochure from the hotel?

i. Isn't there _ _ _ _ _ _ who could tell me the way to Cumberland?

j. I know _ _ _ _ _ _, but he is not here at the moment.

k. Did _ _ _ _ _ _ call me last night?

l. Yes, _ _ _ _ _ _ did, but I forgot her name.

m. Do you know _ _ _ _ _ _ who speaks Chinese?

n. No, I don't know _ _ _ _ _ _.

o. Did _ _ _ _ _ _ see my dog?

84. MAKE A CHOICE Welche Form ist richtig? Kreisen Sie sie ein!

a. She **has spoken to me/has been speaking to me** three times today.

b. I have just **cut/been cutting** my foot.

c. He **has written /has been writing** letters all morning.

d. We **have owned/have been owning** this car for five years.

e. **Have you ever been/have you been going** to Rome?

f. Last week, we **saw/have seen** the Queen.

g. They **lived/have lived** here since last year.

h. They **moved/have moved** here one year ago.

i. The day before yesterday, the weather **was/has been** horrible.

j. He **was/has been** here many times recently.

k. When **did you go/have you been** to Egypt?

l. **Did you ever go/have you ever been** to Italy?

m. **Was she/has she been** here last week?

n. **Did you see/have you seen** him yet?

o. How long **did you live/have you lived** in Germany when you were a child?

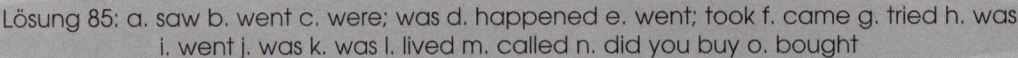

Lösung 85: a. saw b. went c. were; was d. happened e. went; took f. came g. tried h. was
i. went j. was k. was l. lived m. called n. did you buy o. bought

85. SIMPLE PAST Vervollständigen Sie die Sätze!

a. I _ _ _ _ _ Judy this morning on my way to school.

b. Yesterday Tim, Sally and I _ _ _ _ _ to the cinema.

c. When _ _ _ _ _ you there? - I _ _ _ _ _ there at six o'clock.

d. It _ _ _ _ _ fifteen minutes ago at the supermarket.

e. We _ _ _ _ _ to Italy last year.

f. Yesterday afternoon our aunt Nelly _ _ _ _ _ to visit us.

g. I _ _ _ _ _ to get a last minute ticket to Los Angeles in vain.

h. Two days ago there _ _ _ _ _ a big storm outside.

i. In 1976 we _ _ _ _ _ on holiday with some friends.

j. The train _ _ _ _ _ twenty minutes late.

k. Dorothy's twenty-seventh birthday _ _ _ _ _ yesterday.

l. They _ _ _ _ _ in Germany for twenty years.

m. One hour ago somebody _ _ _ _ _ here for you.

n. Where _ _ _ _ _ the nice shirt you gave to Sally?

o. Oh, I _ _ _ _ _ it in Spain.

sah
gingen
warst; war
passierte
fuhren
kam
versuchte
war
fuhren
war
war
lebten
rief an
hast du gekauft
kaufte

86. ARTICLE OR NO ARTICLE? Wo muss der bestimmte oder unbestimmte Artikel stehen?

a. I was born on _ _ _ _ _ first of March.

b. _ _ _ _ _ pity that such _ _ _ _ _ talented girl should drop out of school.

c. I would not do that for all _ _ _ _ _ money in the world.

d. It was such _ _ _ _ _ bad film that I left early.

e. It is too nice _ _ _ _ _ _ _ _ _ day not to go swimming.

f. "What _ _ _ _ _ goal", shouted the commentator when the ball hit the net.

g. Our teacher was sick for quite _ _ _ _ _ while last winter.

h. He bought half _ _ _ _ _ pint of cream in the shop.

i. That is too dangerous _ _ _ _ _ journey in this weather.

j. This is quite _ _ _ _ _ easy exercise to begin with.

k. Both _ _ _ _ _ boy and his friend left the train at Wembley.

l. Half _ _ _ _ _ class was absent on Tuesday because of the icy roads.

m. What is _ _ _ _ _ highest mountain in the world?

n. His house is twice _ _ _ _ _ size of ours.

o. That was so easy _ _ _ _ _ test I was finished before the time was up.

Lösung 87: a. not as; as b. than c. as; as d. as; as e. than f. than g. as; as h. not as; as i. than j. as; as k. than l. not as; as m. than n. than o. as; as

Lösung 86: a. on the b. what a pity; such a c. all the d. such a e. too nice a f. what a g. quite a
h. half a i. too dangerous a j. quite an k. both the l. half the m. the highest n. twice the
o. so easy a

87. AS, NOT AS, NOT SO, OR THAN Was muss in der Lücke stehen?

a. What a pity the weather was _ _ _ _ nice today _ _ _ _ yesterday.

b. Munich is a far bigger city _ _ _ _ Nuremberg.

c. Stephen paid _ _ _ _ much money _ _ _ _ Carol for his ticket.

d. The River Thames is _ _ _ _ long _ _ _ _ the Danube.

e. In my opinion Brecht was a far better dramatist _ _ _ _ Beckett.

f. Colin awoke earlier _ _ _ _ the rest of us.

g. If she is _ _ _ _ attractive _ _ _ _ you say she must be a lovely girl.

h. Scotland is _ _ _ _ warm _ _ _ _ Italy.

i. French is much harder _ _ _ _ English.

j. Is it _ _ _ _ difficult an exercise _ _ _ _ you thought?

k. Actually it's harder _ _ _ _ I expected.

l. I'm afraid he's _ _ _ _ good _ _ _ _ he used to be.

m. Tim is much more handsome _ _ _ _ his brother.

n. Is Mount Everest higher _ _ _ _ Mount McKinley?

o. The car is not running _ _ _ _ well _ _ _ _ it usually does.

88. FILL IN THE BLANK Vervollständigen Sie die Sätze!

a. What **have you been doing/are you been doing** for the last few days?

b. When we arrived **it was snowing/it snowed**.

c. Has he arrived **just/yet**?

d. We **have been having/used to have** a computer.

e. **Someone/Anyone** came to our place yesterday.

f. She speaks English **beautiful/beautifully**.

g. He cuts his fingernails once **in the month/a month**.

h. I often go **in/to** the cinema.

i. - She likes beer. - **So I do/So do I**.

j. No, that's not **necessary/necessarily**.

k. This man is **more intelligent/intelligenter** than me.

l. I'll do my work **morning/tomorrow**.

m. **Whose/Who's** book is this?

n. **I am wanting/I want** to invite him out for dinner.

o. What time **it is/is it**?

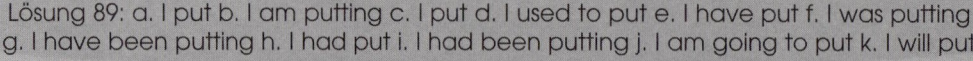

Lösung 89: a. I put b. I am putting c. I put d. I used to put e. I have put f. I was putting
g. I have been putting h. I had put i. I had been putting j. I am going to put k. I will put

Lösung 88: a. have you been doing b. it was snowing c. yet d. used to have e. Someone
f. beautifully g. a month h. to i. So do I j. necessary k. more intelligent l. tomorrow m. Whose
n. I want o. is it

89. PUT IT BLUNTLY Geben Sie die richtigen Formen an!

I / to put

a. *einfache Gegenwart:* _____

b. *Verlaufsform der Gegenwart:* _____

c. *einfache Vergangenheit:* _____

d. *Vergangenheit mit „used to":* _____

e. *Verlaufsform der Vergangenheit:* _____

f. *present perfect:* _____

g. *Verlaufsform des present perfect:* _____

h. *Plusquamperfekt:* _____

i. *Verlaufsform des Plusquamperfekts:* _____

j. *Zukunft mit „will":* _____

k. *Zukunft mit „going to":* _____

l. *future perfect:* _____

m. *Verlaufsform des future perfect:* _____

90. SOFT, SOFTLY Wie heißen die Adverbien dieser Adjektive?

a. good -------------------------------------➤
b. crazy -------------------------------------➤
c. selfish ------------------------------------➤
d. silent -------------------------------------➤
e. incredible ---------------------------------➤
f. ecstatic -----------------------------------➤
g. stunning -----------------------------------➤
h. mild --------------------------------------➤
i. brave -------------------------------------➤
j. eager -------------------------------------➤
k. lame --------------------------------------➤
l. petulant -----------------------------------➤
m. shy ---------------------------------------➤
n. uncanny -----------------------------------➤
o. basic --------------------------------------➤

Lösung 91: a. on b. for c. of d. for e. of f. to g. to h. on i. of j. to; about k. at l. about m. of n. for o. on/along

Lösung 90: a. well b. crazily c. selfishly d. silently e. incredibly f. ecstatically g. stunningly
h. mildly i. bravely j. eagerly k. lamely l. petulantly m. shyly n. uncannily
o. basically

91. THINK ABOUT IT Setzen Sie die richtige Präposition ein!

a. Gerard insisted _ _ _ _ _ paying for the meal.

b. We sent _ _ _ _ _ the doctor the minute he fell ill.

c. My father makes good use _ _ _ _ _ his artistic skills.

d. Terry asked me _ _ _ _ _ some money.

e. I am getting very tired _ _ _ _ _ these delays.

f. Eileen delivered the letter _ _ _ _ _ the company for me.

g. He explained it very well _ _ _ _ _ me.

h. Can I rely _ _ _ _ _ you to do that?

i. What do you think _ _ _ _ _ my new suit?

j. Do I need to speak _ _ _ _ _ him _ _ _ _ _ the matter?

k. Why are they laughing _ _ _ _ _ us?

l. I've heard a lot _ _ _ _ _ his new play.

m. Helen does not think much _ _ _ _ _ her chances in the election.

n. I'm waiting _ _ _ _ _ Patrick.

o. Jack gets _ _ _ _ _ well with everyone.

92. CHOOSE WISELY Wählen Sie den richtigen Begriff aus!

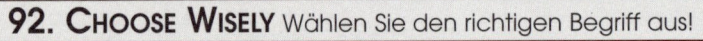

a. I don't have **many/much** time.

b. I **would like/I will** a pound of bananas, please.

c. **Can I have/Can I has** a glass of water, please?

d. I **have ridden/used to ride** my bicycle, but now I walk to work.

e. Where **find I/can I find** the station?

f. Turn left **at/on** the traffic light.

g. At the moment he **is reading/reads**.

h. She's got **some/any** sweets.

i. How old **is/are** you?

j. Nina is good **at/in** swimming.

k. A: Where does she come from? B: She's from **Italy/Italian**.

l. **Everyone/anyone** is already here.

m. Angus sends his **greets/regards**.

n. **Has/have** you seen the tigers yet?

o. They run very **slowly/slow**.

Lösung 93: a. would speak b. can c. would get d. were e. had not forgotten f. rises g. asked h. would have met i. could help j. had known, could have told k. would have passed, had studied l. blows m. could take n. had come o. would get

93. IF-CLAUSES Setzen Sie die Verben in der passenden Form ein!

a. If he lived in Dublin, he _ _ _ _ better English.

b. We _ _ _ _ take the bus to work if the weather is bad.

c. If I sold my house in Knightsbridge I _ _ _ _ at least a million for it.

d. If John _ _ _ _ old enough, he would marry Susan.

e. If they _ _ _ _ to post the letter, the school might have got it by now.

f. Will we have to move upstairs if the river _ _ _ _?

g. If you _ _ _ _ him, he would help you.

h. If Connie had known you were coming, she _ _ _ _ you at the station.

i. It would be just great if you _ _ _ _ me.

j. If I _ _ _ _ what time the train was leaving last night I _ _ _ _ you.

k. The students _ _ _ _ their exams this time if they _ _ _ _ harder.

l. If the wind _ _ _ _ any harder it will knock the old oak down.

m. It would be nice if you _ _ _ _ me with you.

n. If they _ _ _ _ we would have spent a nice evening together.

o. If I sold this car, I _ _ _ _ at least $500 for it.

speak
can
get
be
not forget
rise
ask
meet
help
know; tell
pass; study
blow
take
come
get

94. PASSIVE Bilden Sie das Passiv in der angegebenen Zeit!

a.	She (coach) by a famous tennis player.	*Present Continuous*
b.	My car (steal) by someone.	*Present Perfect*
c.	The letter (post) in Manchester.	*Simple Past*
d.	The animals (feed) every evening.	*Simple Present*
e.	He (transport) to prison at the time.	*Past Continuous*
f.	The slippers (find) in the attic.	*Simple Past*
g.	The ice-cream (make) when we arrived.	*Past Continuous*
h.	It (eat) tonight.	*will-Futur*
i.	The floor (scrub) by the cleaning ladies.	*Present Continuous*
j.	The furniture (deliver) by the firm.	*Past Perfect*
k.	Don't look now, but I think we (follow).	*Present Continuous*
l.	The lawn (mow) by Leon tomorrow.	*will-Futur*
m.	Max thought his talents (waste).	*Past Continuous*
n.	The names in the story (change).	*Present Perfect*
o.	We (serve) by the most attentive waitress.	*Present Continuous*

Lösung 95: a. has been sneezing b. has caught c. has taken d. have been cutting
e. has had f. Has Sean eaten g. have bought h. have been i. has been helping
j. has Kevin been doing k. has gone l. has he been getting up to? m. have not received
n. have been lying o. has climbed

Lösung 94: a. is being coached b. has been stolen c. was posted d. are fed
e. was being transported f. were found g. was being made h. will be eaten i. is being scrubbed
j. had been delivered k. are being followed l. will be mowed/mown m. were being wasted
n. have been changed o. are being served

95. PRESENT PERFECT OR PRESENT PERFECT CONTINUOUS? Wählen Sie die Verbform aus!

a. Sean _ _ _ _ _ _ a great deal of late.

b. He _ _ _ _ _ _ a cold, I'm sure of it.

c. I don't think so. Mary _ _ _ _ _ _ his temperature and it's normal.

d. Maybe it's hay fever. They _ _ _ _ _ _ the hay all week.

e. Possibly, but he _ _ _ _ _ _ his shots this year.

f. Sean _ _ _ _ _ _ anything unusual recently?

g. No, but we _ _ _ _ _ _ new carpets.

h. That might _ _ _ _ _ _ it.

i. He _ _ _ _ _ _ me clean the old ones all week.

j. What Kevin _ _ _ _ _ _ this past while?

k. Kevin _ _ _ _ _ _ to England for the holidays.

l. And what he _ _ _ _ _ _ up to?

m. God only knows. We _ _ _ _ _ _ a letter or phone call since he left.

n. You _ _ _ _ _ _ to me all this time, you louse!

o. Andy _ _ _ _ _ _ Mount Everest twice and lived to tell about it.

sneeze
catch
take
cut
have
eat
bought
be
help
do
go
get
not/receive
lie
climb

96. RING, RANG, RUNG Fügen Sie die Stammformen dieser Verben ein!

a. become, _____ become
b. _____ broke, broken
c. cling, _____ clung
d. _____ drew, drawn
e. hit, hit, _____
f. leave, _____ left
g. _____ met, met
h. ring, rang, _____

i. sew, _____ sewn
j. slit, slit, _____
k. spring, _____ sprung
l. _____ stood, stood
m. _____ taught, taunght
n. wake, woke, _____
o. wear, wore, _____

Lösung 97: a. going b. in trying c. of getting d. of giving e. to take f. on using; being
g. bringing; transporting; to take h. to spending i. of listening j. talking, on washing; to drink.

97. FILL IN THE BLANK Setzen Sie die passenden Verbformen ein!

a. How about _ _ _ _ _ camping this weekend? — **to go**

b. I'm interested _ _ _ _ _ it. — **to try**

c. Is there any chance _ _ _ _ _ the car from Dad? — **to get**

d. No way, he wouldn't dream _ _ _ _ _ it to us. — **to give**

e. Would you like _ _ _ _ _ the bus? — **to take**

f. No, I'm not keen _ _ _ _ _ the bus, I hate _ _ _ _ _ so cramped. — **to use; to be**

g. Would you mind me _ _ _ _ _ Anna along? She's got a car, then we — **to bring**
wouldn't have to worry about _ _ _ _ _ all the — **to transport**
things we want _ _ _ _ _ with us. — **to take**

h. Good idea! I am looking forward _ _ _ _ _ some time away from — **to spend**
our parents.

i. I am sick _ _ _ _ _ to them all the time. — **to listen**

j. Mum never stops _ _ _ _ _ and Dad goes _ _ _ _ _ his car all Saturday, — **to talk; to wash**
he doesn't even stop _ _ _ _ _ a cup of tea! — **to drink**

98. PASSIVE Bilden Sie das Passiv in der angegebenen Zeit!

a.	The bulding (pull down).	*Present Perfect*
b.	The game (play) in Newcastle.	*Present Continuous*
c.	The sofa (design) by John Jones.	*Simple Past*
d.	She (bring) to the hotel by helicopter.	*Present Perfect*
e.	The post (deliver) each day.	*Simple Present*
f.	The operation (do) at a London clinic.	*Present Continuous*
g.	The clinic (build) in 1989.	*Simple Past*
h.	A new head (appoint) next year.	*will-Futur*
i.	A policeman (attack) in Watford.	*Present Perfect*
j.	The Queen (show) the new school.	*Simple Past*
k.	The song (write) by an English girl.	*Simple Past*
l.	It (sing) by a famous tenor.	*will-Futur*
m.	The book (publish) by Faber and Faber.	*Present Perfect*
n.	The robber (report) to the police.	*Simple Past*
o.	The windows (clean) by the woman.	*Past Perfect*

Lösung 99: a. ... wouldn't be there b. ... wanted to go c. ... didn't want to hear it
d. ... should give them back e. ... was a planet f. ... might do it g. ... could afford it
h. ... had told him about it i. ... might have done it j. ... had never been there

99. WHO SAID THAT? Bilden Sie die indirekte Rede.

a. "I won't be there."

b. "Do you want to go?"

c. "I don't want to hear it."

d. "Please give them back."

e. "Mars is a planet."

f. "We may do it."

g. "I can afford it."

h. "Max told me about it."

i. "Colin may have done it."

j. "We've never been there."

a. Mr. Jacobs told me that he _____

b. Eric asked me if I _____

c. My friend said that he _____

d. Wesley said that I _____

e. Dr. Birrell pointed out that Mars _____

f. Richard mentioned today that they _____

g. Prescott boasted that he _____

h. Bernard admitted that Max _____

i. Anne suggested that Colin _____

j. Audrey insisted that they _____

100. IF ONLY ... Verbinden Sie Bedingung oder Folge mit der passenden Verbform!

a. I _ _ _ _ _ here if I had known that he wasn't here.

b. I _ _ _ _ _ to Hawaii this year if I have enough money.

c. If David were to find out about this, he _ _ _ _ _ very angry.

d. If I _ _ _ _ _ Brian I wouldn't talk to professors in that manner.

e. If you work hard, you _ _ _ _ _ .

f. If you worked harder, you _ _ _ _ _ .

g. Parker won't do it if he _ _ _ _ _ that it's a waste of time.

h. If he had invested wisely ten years ago he _ _ _ _ _ rich today.

i. If the weather _ _ _ _ _ unpleasant we might decide to cancel our trip.

j. If he had missed his bus he _ _ _ _ _ us.

k. If I had thought it over, I _ _ _ _ _ the right choice.

l. If he asks her for a date, she _ _ _ _ _ sure to say yes.

m. He won't do it if you don't _ _ _ _ _ him.

n. If I had known the answer, I wouldn't _ _ _ _ _ .

o. If you read the paper you _ _ _ _ _ what's going on.

to come
to go
to be
to be
to succeed
to succeed
to decide
to be
to be
to call
to make
to be
to pay
to ask
to know

Lösung 101: a. met b. has broken c. shattered d. have you locked e. bolted f. spoke; left
g. have they made h. have you got i. received j. has she ever been k. visited
l. have you ever eaten m. ate n. have you attended o. were; arrived

Lösung 100: a. wouldn't have come b. will go c. would be d. were e. will succeed
f. would succeed g. decides h. would be i. is j. would have called k. would have made
l. will be m. pay n. have asked o. would know

101. SIMPLE PAST OR PRESENT PERFECT? Wie heißt die richtige Verbform?

a. Denise _ _ _ _ _ _ your uncle last Friday. — **meet**

b. Joan _ _ _ _ _ _ four windows since she started playing baseball. — **break**

c. The last one she _ _ _ _ _ _ was in the living room. — **shatter**

d. You _ _ _ _ _ _ the front gate? — **lock**

e. I don't need to. I _ _ _ _ _ _ it yesterday evening. — **bolt**

f. Charles _ _ _ _ _ _ to his wife the night before she _ _ _ _ _ _. — **speak; leave**

g. They _ _ _ _ _ _ ice cream? — **make**

h. You _ _ _ _ _ _ many relatives in the area? — **get**

i. I got two presents. Last Christmas I _ _ _ _ _ _ far more. — **receive**

j. She ever _ _ _ _ _ _ to Greece? — **be**

k. She _ _ _ _ _ _ the country as a child. — **visit**

l. You ever _ _ _ _ _ _ bacon and cabbage? — **eat**

m. Yes, I _ _ _ _ _ _ it when I was in Scotland. — **eat**

n. And you _ _ _ _ _ _ the Highland Games? — **attend**

o. Unfortunately not. They _ _ _ _ _ _ over by the time we _ _ _ _ _ _. — **be; arrive**

102. WHERE'S THE SUBJECT? Kreisen Sie das Subjekt des Satzes ein!

a. I think that there is no country more beautiful than Austria.
b. According to many people, fishing is the most relaxing of all hobbies.
c. One must admit that Robertson has improved his performance since last year.
d. Eric and Lawrence are my closest friends.
e. Andy is the one whom I trusted the most.
f. There is nothing to worry about.
g. "That's a matter of opinion," I replied.
h. Nobody noticed her new hairstyle.
i. Of all the people who started the marathon, only eight made it to the finish line.
j. Bob Johnson, our chairman, has called a staff meeting for this afternoon.
k. The news made me happy.
l. I called my brother a liar.
m. You must admit he's got a point.
n. Rumour has it that he's engaged.
o. Although she's very friendly, I don't like her.

Lösung 103: a. ... wares there b. ... played well ... c. ... just a young boy ... d. Fortunately, the damage ... e. I always exercise ... f. ... extremely angry g. ... come here today h. ... stroll after work/After work I like ... i. ... was quite pleasant j. .. completely finished k. We never discuss ... l. Luckily, I was able ... m. ... Bible twice n. ... job well o. ... easy enough ...

103. ADVERBS Wo müssen die Adverbien stehen?

a. Merchants sell their wares.
b. Manfred played in yesterday's game.
c. Although he was a young boy, he knew quite a lot.
d. The damage was not serious.
e. I exercise when I get up in the morning.
f. One could see that she was angry.
g. I wish I hadn't come here.
h. I like to go for a stroll.
i. Sammy's journey was pleasant.
j. The job is now finished.
k. We discuss business during dinner.
l. I was able to understand most of it.
m. Chris has read the entire Bible.
n. Alex did his job.
o. The textbook is easy to understand.

there
well
just
fortunately
always
extremely
today
after work
quite
completely
never
luckily
twice
well
enough

104. INDIRECT SPEECH Bilden Sie die indirekte Rede!

a. Crystal City have signed a new striker.
b. We are going to Brazil on our holidays.
c. He wrote to Alison last month.
d. The film had a very sad ending.
e. The sheep were shorn earlier last year.
f. If you're back in time we can take in a film.
g. Father Smith must be sick.
h. There will be trouble if my parents find out.
i. Fiona should have worked harder.
j. I wanted a break last year but didn't get one.
k. Harry knows all sorts of witty expressions.
l. Mechanics are famous for overcharging.
m. Cheryl is too lazy to make much of an effort.
n. The water is freezing cold.
o. I need some time to think it over.

a. I knew that Crystal City _____
b. They said that they _____
c. He told me that he _____
d. I told you that the film _____
e. She said that the sheep _____
f. He said that if I _____
g. He said that Father Smith _____
h. Sharon said that there _____
i. Mike knew that Fiona _____
j. He said that he _____
k. Jo told me that Harry _____
l. Woody said that mechanics _____
m. Dave said that Cheryl _____
n. Nathan said the water_____
o. Tom said he _____

Lösung 105: a. bent b. bring c. come d. drunk e. fled f. gave g. held h. lent i. paid j. rose k. shook l. sat m. speak n. strung o. tear

105. GO, WENT, GONE Wie heißen die Stammformen?

a. bend, bent, _____

b. _____, brought, brought

c. come, came, _____

d. drink, drank, _____

e. flee, fled, _____

f. give, _____, given

g. hold, held, _____

h. lend, lent, _____

i. pay, _____, paid

j. rise, _____, risen

k. shake, _____, shaken

l. sit, sat, _____

m. _____, spoke, spoken

n. string, _____, strung

o. _____, tore, torn

106. SINGULAR OR PLURAL? Welches englische Wort gehört in die Lücke?

a. The news _ _ _ _ _ _ depressing.   *sein*
b. Where are you going to put the_ _ _ _ _ _ ?   *Möbel*
c. John has broken his _ _ _ _ _ _ .   *Brille*
d. Bronchitis _ _ _ _ _ _ not very pleasant.   *sein*
e. It is sometimes difficult to find _ _ _ _ _ _ in London.   *Unterkünfte*
f. Elizabeth is busy doing her _ _ _ _ _ _ .   *Hausaufgaben*
g. John was very impressed by the beautiful _ _ _ _ _ _ .   *Umgebung*
h. Fred gave me some good _ _ _ _ _ _ .   *Ratschläge*
i. Have you seen my _ _ _ _ _ _ ?   *Hose*
j. The United Nations _ _ _ _ _ _ very busy.   *sein*
k. Could you give me some _ _ _ _ _ _ .   *Informationen*
l. Where do you get your _ _ _ _ _ _ cut?   *Haare*
m. Glasses _ _ _ _ _ _ ugly compared to contact lenses.   *sein*
n. His counsel _ _ _ _ _ _ much appreciated.   *sein*
o. The rooms _ _ _ _ _ _ comfortable but not luxurious.   *sein*

Lösung 107: a. have been waiting b. has been studying c. have been washing d. have been doing e. has been sleeping f. have been trying g. haven't been feeling h. have been playing i. has been doing the laundry j. have been standing k. has been raining l. haven't been working m. have been eating n. have been wanting o. has been yawning

107. PRESENT PERFECT CONTINUOUS Setzen Sie die richtige Verbform ein!

a. I _ _ _ _ _ _ _ for you for two hours. — **wait**

b. She _ _ _ _ _ _ _ English for four years. — **study**

c. I _ _ _ _ _ _ _ the dishes all morning. — **wash**

d. We _ _ _ _ _ _ _ a lot since the weather's got warm. — **do**

e. He _ _ _ _ _ _ _ since 7 o'clock last night. — **sleep**

f. I _ _ _ _ _ _ _ to talk to you for weeks. — **try**

g. You _ _ _ _ _ _ _ well lately. — **not feel**

h. We _ _ _ _ _ _ _ all afternoon. — **play**

i. He _ _ _ _ _ _ _ since six o'clock. — **do the laundry**

j. They _ _ _ _ _ _ _ at this bus stop for thirty minutes. — **stand**

k. It _ _ _ _ _ _ _ all week. — **rain**

l. You _ _ _ _ _ _ _ today. — **not work**

m. We _ _ _ _ _ _ _ at this restaurant for years. — **eat**

n. They _ _ _ _ _ _ _ to tidy up the flat for a long time. — **want**

o. Jeff _ _ _ _ _ _ _ during the entire lecture. — **yawn**

108. IF ONLY ... Setzen Sie die Verben in der passenden Form ein.

a. They would not have lost the match if the goalkeeper _ _ _ _ better. — *play*

b. If Anita had heard you were in town she _ _ _ _ you. — *ring*

c. Had the car not been travelling so fast Sean _ _ _ _ a chance. — *have*

d. Terry and Tina were invited to a dance; otherwise they _ _ _ _ us. — *accompany*

e. If their car had not broken down they _ _ _ _ here earlier. — *break*

f. If the warranty _ _ _ _ out I could have got the tea. — *not run*

g. Harper would not have back pain if he _ _ _ _ his exercises. — *do*

h. He would be rich by now if he _ _ _ _ his money wisely. — *invest*

i. Charlie _ _ _ _ long ago if he had found the right girl. — *marry*

j. If you _ _ _ _ harder he might have been pleased with you. — *work*

k. If I _ _ _ _ right away, I would have had to fight the traffic. — *leave*

l. If Ann _ _ _ _ what I told her to do, she wouldn't have got in trouble. — *do*

m. If John had told her what he really thought, she _ _ _ _ him. — *slap*

n. If you had read the book, you _ _ _ _ better on the test. — *do*

o. If my alarm clock had worked I _ _ _ _ up on time. — *wake*

Lösung 109: a. going to b. will c. will d. going to e. 're going to f. I'll have g. we'll h. won't oder is not going to i. I'll j. I'm going to k. is going to l. is going to m. will n. is going to o. will

Lösung 108: a. had played b. would have rung c. would have had d. would have accompanied
e. would have been f. had not run g. had done h. had invested i. would have married
j. had worked k. had left l. had done m. would have slapped n. would have done
o. would have woken

109. WILL OR GOING TO Wählen Sie die passendste Form aus!

a. Look at those big black clouds! It **is going to/will** rain!

b. The sun **is going to/will** shine next summer.

c. I hope it'**s going to be/will** be a nice day tomorrow.

d. He's hungry, he'**s going to/will** eat something.

e. Do you have plans for the summer? Yes. We'**re going go /'ll** go to Spain.

f. I think **I'm going to have/I'll have** the chicken.

g. Perhaps **we're going to/we'll** go to the pub tonight.

h. Surely it'**s not going to/won't** happen.

i. Oh, no. It's raining! **I'm going to/I'll** roll up the windows of my car

j. Oh, no. I'm late! **I'm going to/I'll** miss the bus.

k. Sally **is going to/will** have a baby.

l. Ralph **is going to/will** spend Christmas in Hawaii.

m. The funeral **is going to/will** be held in Yuma.

n. He **is going to/will** mess it up - I'm sure of it.

o. It **is going to/will** get dark around 7 p.m.

110. COMPLETE THE SENTENCES Setzen Sie das Adverb an die richtige Stelle!

a. I have liked Tom.
b. Karen and Stephanie were feeling tired.
c. The game was abandoned.
d. The planned project was a failure.
e. I recall my first teacher.
f. Kevin bought a second car.
g. Sharon has a shower in the morning.
h. Has Kelly gone to work with you?
i. James had done his homework when he went to a party.
j. He had finished when I rang.
k. The private funeral was attended by many journalists.
l. He drinks beer.
m. You have answered the question.

always
probably
immediately
expensively
clearly
foolishly
usually
ever
hardly
almost
strictly
seldom
correctly

Lösung 111: a. Did Sara write b. hasn't got c. helped d. have shorn e. saved f. drove; was g. made h. found i. has passed; has started j. has vanished k. has improved l. shone m. said; was n. hasn't spoken o. damaged

Lösung 110: a. have always b. probably feeling/probably were c. immediately abandoned/ abandoned immediately d. expensively planned e. clearly recall/teacher clearly f. foolishly bought/Foolishly, Kevin .. g. usually has/Usually, Sharon .. h. ever gone i. Hardly has James/has hardly done j. almost had/had almost k. strictly private l. seldom drinks m. question correctly

111. SIMPLE PAST OR PRESENT PERFECT? Notieren Sie die richtige Verbform!

a. Sara _ _ _ _ _ _ to the Prime Minister?	write
b. Yes, but she _ _ _ _ _ _ a reply yet.	not/get
c. Rick _ _ _ _ _ _ his father with the work last year.	help
d. The men _ _ _ _ _ _ many sheep so far this summer.	shear
e. The little girl _ _ _ _ _ _ a lot of money last year.	save
f. Bill never _ _ _ _ _ _ a car until he _ _ _ _ _ _ 18.	drive/be
g. The Queen of Hearts _ _ _ _ _ _ some tarts all on a summer's day.	make
h. Rosie _ _ _ _ _ _ the exam too difficult yesterday.	find
i. She _ _ _ _ _ _ every exam since she _ _ _ _ _ _ college.	pass; start
j. Mark _ _ _ _ _ _! We can't find him.	vanish
k. The weather here _ _ _ _ _ _ greatly.	improve
l. The sun _ _ _ _ _ _ the whole day yesterday.	shine
m. And last night the weatherman _ _ _ _ _ _ the outlook _ _ _ _ _ good.	say; be
n. Jeremy _ _ _ _ _ _ _ _ _ _ to her since the break up.	not/speak
o. The children _ _ _ _ _ _ the Mercedes last Sunday afternoon.	damage

112. WRITE, WROTE, HAVE WRITTEN Setzen Sie die fehlenden Stammformen ein!

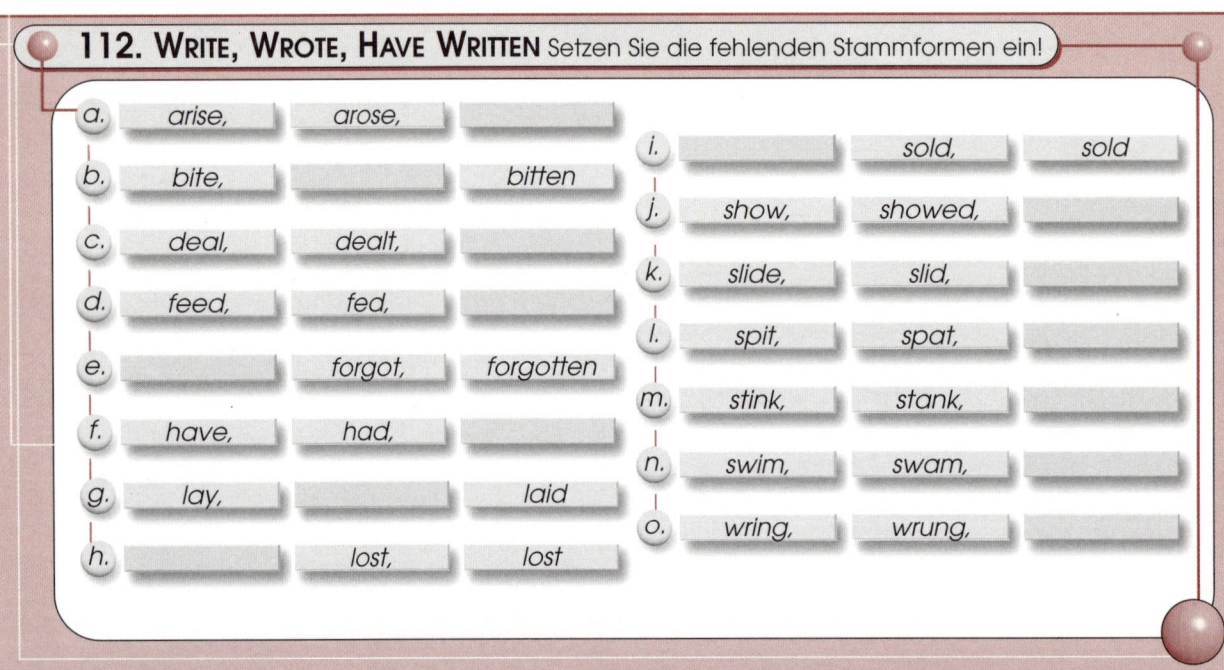

a. arise, arose, _____

b. bite, _____, bitten

c. deal, dealt, _____

d. feed, fed, _____

e. _____, forgot, forgotten

f. have, had, _____

g. lay, _____, laid

h. _____, lost, lost

i. _____, sold, sold

j. show, showed, _____

k. slide, slid, _____

l. spit, spat, _____

m. stink, stank, _____

n. swim, swam, _____

o. wring, wrung, _____

Lösung 113: a. was bought b. will be written c. will be done d. was made e. is being criticized
f. was visited g. was given h. will be walked i. is being eaten j. will be opened k. have been sold
l. has been ridden m. will be painted n. were told o. were turned out

113. QUESTIONS ARE BEING ANSWERED Wie lauten die Passivformen?

a. I bought a coat.
b. She will write the report.
c. Someone will do the work.
d. Mr. Smith made the coffee.
e. We are criticizing Bernie.
f. The Prime Minister visited the museum.
g. Geoffrey gave me this book.
h. We will walk the dog.
i. We are eating dinner.
j. The firm will open a new office tomorrow.
k. We have sold some books.
l. He has ridden a horse.
m. We will paint our house in the summer.
n. Steve told us to leave.
o. Carrie turned out the lights.

a. A coat_____
b. The report_____
c. The work _____
d. The coffee _____
e. Bernie _____
f. The museum _____
g. The book _____
h. The dog _____
i. Dinner_____
j. A new office_____
k. Some books _____
l. A horse_____
m. Our house_____
n. We _____
o. The lights_____

114. CONTINGENCY PLANS Setzen Sie die richtige Form ein!

a. We won't go hiking if it _ _ _ _ _ _.   **rain**
b. If I see Robert, I _ _ _ _ _ _ him.   **ask**
c. If we have time, we _ _ _ _ _ _ to the mountains.   **go**
d. You won't be so tired if you _ _ _ _ _ _ more sleep.   **get**
e. If we miss the train, we _ _ _ _ _ _ to work.   **cycle**
f. What will we do if he _ _ _ _ _ _ late?   **be**
g. If we don't stop now, we _ _ _ _ _ _ the view.   **miss**
h. If there are any problems, will you _ _ _ _ _ _ me?   **phone**
i. You'll get there on time if you _ _ _ _ _ _ a taxi.   **take**
j. If we have enough time at the weekend, we _ _ _ _ _ _ my aunt. **visit**
k. I'll tell him if I _ _ _ _ _ _ him.   **see**
l. What will you do if you _ _ _ _ _ _ your toothbrush?   **forget**
m. We will go skiing this winter if it _ _ _ _ _ _.   **snow**
n. If they ask me, I _ _ _ _ _ _ them some help.   **give**
o. You'll get a good grade if you _ _ _ _ _ _ hard enough.   **study**

Lösung 115: a. twice b. Spanish c. I'm reading d. many; did e. rooms f. loaves g. older h. your i. elder j. Don't k. doing l. working m. Why n. studied o. Were you

Lösung 114: a. rains b. will ask c. will go d. get e. will cycle f. is g. will miss h. phone i. take j. will visit k. see l. forget m. snows n. will give o. study

115. FILL IN THE BLANK Setzen Sie die richtige Form ein!

a. I take the bus every Monday and every Wednesday - that's _ _ _ _ _ _ a week.

b. Is your friend Carmen from Spain? Yes, she's _ _ _ _ _ _.

c. Did you read the book last week? No, _ _ _ _ _ _ it right now.

d. How _ _ _ _ _ _ records _ _ _ _ _ _ you sell yesterday?

e. How many _ _ _ _ _ _ does your flat have?

f. Would you like a loaf of bread? No, one's not enough - I'd like two _ _ _ _ _ _.

g. Neil is five years old and Tom is seven. Tom is two years _ _ _ _ _ _ than Neil.

h. This must be _ _ _ _ _ _ book. Your name is in it.

i. Steve was there, and his _ _ _ _ _ _ brother Tom was there too.

j. The film starts at eight o'clock p.m. _ _ _ _ _ _ be late!

k. What is her new boyfriend _ _ _ _ _ _ for a living at the moment?

l. He is _ _ _ _ _ _ as a shop assistant.

m. _ _ _ _ _ _ did she do that? I don't know the reason.

n. He _ _ _ _ _ _ at Cambridge to become a teacher.

o. Kathy: _ _ _ _ _ _ in London yesterday? Kate: No, I was in Brighton.

116. TRANSLATE Übersetzen Sie die deutschen Begriffe!

a, Stop _ _ _ _ _ _ _ so much! — **reden**

b, The door didn't open so I _ _ _ _ _ _ _ the window. — **probieren**

c, My father _ _ _ _ _ _ _ my bike, so now I can ride it again. — **reparieren**

d, Jason _ _ _ _ _ _ _ his favourite book. Don't disturb him. — **liest**

e, My father _ _ _ _ _ _ _ Japanese for one year now. — **lernen**

f, Who is the girl _ _ _ _ _ _ _ called this morning? — **das**

g, If it _ _ _ _ _ _ _ a little bit warmer today I _ _ _ _ _ _ _ go swimming. — **sein**

h, If somebody _ _ _ _ _ _ _ her she would have been able to succeed. — **helfen**

i, I saw Susan today. She said that she _ _ _ _ _ _ _ on holiday soon. — **fahren**

j, Susan also asked if Mary _ _ _ _ _ _ _ to come with her. — **wollen**

k, What is _ _ _ _ _ _ _ this door? — **hinter**

l, Jeff, _ _ _ _ _ _ _ we _ _ _ _ _ _ yesterday, is a friend of mine. — **den; treffen**

m, She _ _ _ _ _ _ _ at the bus-stop far too long yesterday. — **warten**

n, What _ _ _ _ _ _ _ you do for the next two days? — **werden**

o, I _ _ _ _ _ _ _ go to work tomorrow morning. — **werden**

Lösung 117: a. Americans b. Germans c. Thais d. Australians e. Italians f. Japanese g. Swiss h. English i. Irish j. Scots k. Welsh l. French m. Spaniards n. Czechs o. Chinese

Lösung 116: a. talking b. tried c. has repaired d. is reading e. has been learning f. who
g. were; would h. had helped i. was going j. wanted k. behind l. whom; met m. waited n. will
o. will

117. PEOPLE Wie nennt man das Volk des angegebenen Landes?

a. Amerika: the ---------------------------------- ⤍
b. Deutschland: the ---------------------------------- ⤍
c. Thailand: the ---------------------------------- ⤍
d. Australien: the ---------------------------------- ⤍
e. Italien: the ---------------------------------- ⤍
f. Japan: the ---------------------------------- ⤍
g. Schweiz: the ---------------------------------- ⤍
h. England: the ---------------------------------- ⤍
i. Irland: the ---------------------------------- ⤍
j. Schottland: the ---------------------------------- ⤍
k. Wales: the ---------------------------------- ⤍
l. Frankreich: the ---------------------------------- ⤍
m. Spanien: the ---------------------------------- ⤍
n. Tschechische Republik: the ---------------------------------- ⤍
o. China: the ---------------------------------- ⤍

118. PAST PERFECT Setzen Sie das Verb ins Past Perfect!

a. When we reached Calais the ferry _ _ _ _ _.   *leave*

b. I wasn't thirsty. I just _ _ _ _ _ a beer.   *have*

c. The film was interesting even though I _ _ _ _ _ it before.   *see*

d. The outlaw died at the end after the good guys _ _ _ _ _ him.   *shoot*

e. If you _ _ _ _ _ a raincoat you wouldn't have got drenched.   *bring*

f. John would not have hurt the girl if he _ _ _ _ _ the stone.   *not/throw*

g. I didn't see him the last time I was home. He _ _ _ _ _ away.   *go*

h. By the time Kate reached Heathrow I _ _ _ _ _ transport for her.   *arrange*

i. The explosion at Number 10 clearly _ _ _ _ _ the ministers.   *shake*

j. After the doctor _ _ _ _ _ me the medicine my condition improved.   *give*

k. By the time the police arrived, the burglar _ _ _ _ _ the scene.   *flee*

l. When all was said and done Josh _ _ _ _ _ the roller-coaster ten times.   *ride*

m. Josh and I _ _ _ _ _ in line for so long that our feet were really aching.   *stand*

n. My granddad _ _ _ _ _ his first million by the time he was 39.   *earn*

o. Clayton noticed that the spider _ _ _ _ _ an intricate web.   *spin*

Lösung 119: a. will have b. loses c. drinks d. should see e. likes f. forget g. smoke h. won't be able
i. don't like j. boil k. want l. were m. asks n. want o. hears

Lösung 118: a. had left b. had just had c. had seen d. had shot e. had brought f. had not thrown
g. had gone h. had arranged i. had shaken j. had given k. had fled l. had ridden m. had stood
n. had earned o. had spun

119. IF-CLAUSES Setzen Sie die Verben in der passenden Form ein!

a. If it snows we _ _ _ _ _ _ to stop. **have**

b. The company will collapse if it _ _ _ _ _ _ any more money. **lose**

c. If Dad _ _ _ _ _ _ any more wine he will be ill. **drink**

d. If you _ _ _ _ _ _ him, tell him to go home. **see**

e. He will buy the car if Gavin _ _ _ _ _ _ it. **like**

f. My mother will be angry if they _ _ _ _ _ _ the milk. **forget**

g. You may get lung cancer if you _ _ _ _ _ _. **smoke**

h. Unless the eye drops cure my sore eyes I _ _ _ _ _ _ to work. **not be able**

i. If you _ _ _ _ _ _ my new hair style then buy me a nice hat. **not like**

j. If you _ _ _ _ _ _ the water I'll make the coffee. **boil**

k. If you _ _ _ _ _ _ to be rich don't waste your money. **want**

l. If you _ _ _ _ _ _ smart, you'd listen to Dana's advice. **be**

m. Sheila will give him her opinion if he _ _ _ _ _ _ her. **ask**

n. If you _ _ _ _ _ _ to join me, feel free to sit here. **want**

o. Tony will scream if he _ _ _ _ _ _ that one more time. **hear**

120. "MOST" OR "THE MOST"? Wo gehört der bestimmte Artikel hin und wo nicht?

a. Charlie, like _ _ _ _ _ most of my friends, loves watching football.

b. He gets on with _ _ _ _ _ most people he knows.

c. Last year he met _ _ _ _ _ most exciting woman he had ever seen.

d. _ _ _ _ _ most of _ _ _ _ _ time he couldn't stop thinking of her.

e. After he had spent _ _ _ _ _ most of his money on her, she left him.

f. That was _ _ _ _ _ most miserable day of his life.

g. _ _ _ _ _ most weekends after that he just stayed at home on his own.

h. He read in the paper that most _ _ _ _ _ men dislike figure skating.

i. That made him feel better, but _ _ _ _ _ most of all it brought back his self-confidence.

j. Last weekend he got married to _ _ _ _ _ most charming girl.

k. _ _ _ _ _ most of his family and friends attended the wedding.

l. Neil spent _ _ _ _ _ most of the summer playing tennis.

m. _ _ _ _ _ most people lie at least once a day.

n. Phoebe lies a lot, but she's more honest than _ _ _ _ _ most people.

o. Of all the salesmen Mark was the one who sold _ _ _ _ _ most cars.

Lösung 121: a. bound b. buy c. ate d. fell e. fly f. knew g. lit h. read i. saw j. slept k. spent l. stuck m. swept n. think o. threw

121. IRREGULAR VERBS Setzen Sie die fehlenden Formen ein!

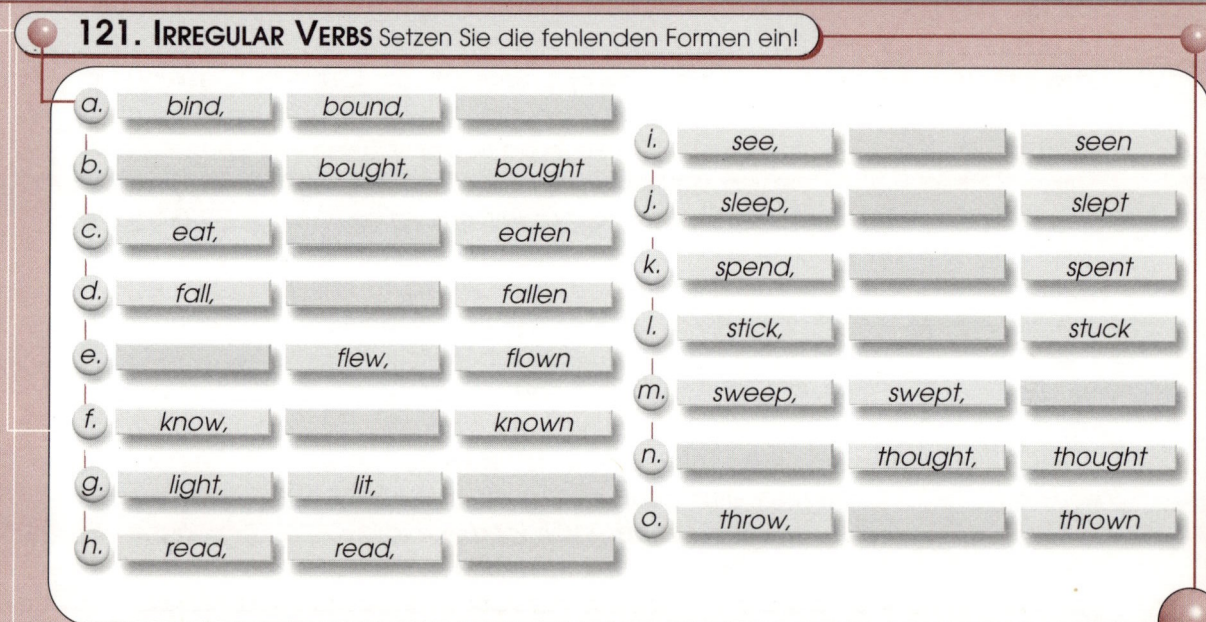

a. *bind,* *bound,*

b. *bought,* *bought*

c. *eat,* *eaten*

d. *fall,* *fallen*

e. *flew,* *flown*

f. *know,* *known*

g. *light,* *lit,*

h. *read,* *read,*

i. *see,* *seen*

j. *sleep,* *slept*

k. *spend,* *spent*

l. *stick,* *stuck*

m. *sweep,* *swept,*

n. *thought,* *thought*

o. *throw,* *thrown*

122. PAST PERFECT CONTINUOUS Setzen Sie die Verben ins Past Perfect Continuous!

a. Scott _ _ _ _ _ for thousands of miles in the bitter cold. **travel**

b. Tess and I _ _ _ _ _ the problem for ages before we solved it. **discuss**

c. The agency _ _ _ _ _ the applicants when the bomb went off. **interview**

d. Sandra _ _ _ _ _ us of her dizzy spells in the months before the attack. **tell**

e. The mob _ _ _ _ _ for over an hour when the police came. **assemble**

f. The sun _ _ _ _ _ all day and we were exhausted. **shine**

g. Tension _ _ _ _ _ in the days prior to the match. **rise**

h. Joanna _ _ _ _ _ the call. **expect**

i. We _ _ _ _ _ forward to the visit and were very disappointed. **look**

j. You _ _ _ _ _ for the phone do you think you would have heard it? **listen**

k. They _ _ _ _ _ for three years when she told him they were through. **date**

l. Jason _ _ _ _ _ for two hours when his father finally arrived. **wait**

m. I wanted to surprise him, but saw that he _ _ _ _ _ me. **expect**

n. The department _ _ _ _ _ a lot of money until I became the boss. **waste**

o. Harriet _ _ _ _ _ nasty rumours until I told her to stop. **spread**

Lösung 123: a. the children's toys b. Charles' daughter c. the boot of the car d. the green-grocer's shop e. my parents' house f. the handle of the cup g. Mr. Harrison's address h. the Smiths' car i. the boy's football j. the twins' birthday k. London's markets l. the passengers' passports m. St. Mary's cathedral n. the roof of the institute o. the index of the map

Lösung 122: a. had been travelling b. had been discussing c. had been interviewing
d. had been telling e. had been assembling f. had been shining g. had been rising
h. had been expecting i. had been looking j. Had you been listening k. had been dating
l. had been waiting m. had been expecting n. had been wasting o. had been spreading

123. WHOSE IS IT? Setzen Sie den „s-Genitiv" oder den „Genitiv mit of" ein.

a. the toys	-	the children	
b. the daughter	-	Charles	
c. the boot	-	the car	
d. the shop	-	the greengrocer	
e. the house	-	my parents	
f. the handle	-	the cup	
g. the address	-	Mr Harrison	
h. the car	-	the Smiths	
i. the football	-	the boy	
j. the birthday	-	the twins	
k. the markets	-	London	
l. the passports	-	the passengers	
m. the cathedral	-	St. Mary	
n. the roof	-	the institute	
o. the index	-	the map	

124. FILL IN THE BLANK Bilden Sie vollständige Sätze!

a. His _ _ _ _ _ _ son was killed in the war.

b. Roger Milla is the _ _ _ _ _ _ man to score in the World Cup.

c. Hof ist _ _ _ _ _ _ to Munich than Berlin.

d. The weather has been much _ _ _ _ _ _ this year than last.

e. That was the _ _ _ _ _ _ hot whiskey I ever drank.

f. We'll take the _ _ _ _ _ _ train. This one doesn't have a bar.

g. Have you heard the _ _ _ _ _ _ news?

h. Jane is to be our _ _ _ _ _ _ boss.

i. The _ _ _ _ _ _ I try the _ _ _ _ _ _ progress I seem to make.

j. Have you got _ _ _ _ _ _ money than Tom?

k. No way. He earns the _ _ _ _ _ _ money of all of us.

l. It is _ _ _ _ _ _ away than I thought.

m. Jane speaks _ _ _ _ _ _ German than her sister.

n. He finished his course in the _ _ _ _ _ _ amount of time required.

o. It took Albert _ _ _ _ _ _ longer to complete the same course.

ältester
älteste
näher
schlechter
schlechteste
späteren
neuesten
nächste
mehr; weniger
mehr
meiste
weiter
weniger
wenigsten
viel

Lösung 125: a. fair footballer b. a far more difficult opponent than c. the prettiest girl d. hardly ever at home e. quite/fairly difficult f. is close to g. have to work hard nowadays h. just come home i. extremely pleased with the result j. when he was abroad k. The Statue of Liberty l. takes the train each day m. straight across the road n. If only I had more time! o. lately

125. TRANSLATE Übersetzen Sie die unterstrichenen Satzteile ins Englische!

a. Er ist ein _fairer Fußballer_.

b. John McEnroe war ein _viel schwierigerer Gegner als_ sein Bruder Patrick.

c. Jane war _das hübscheste Mädchen_ in meiner Klasse.

d. Er ist _fast nie zu Hause_.

e. Die Aufgabe war _ziemlich schwierig_.

f. Watford _liegt nahe bei_ London.

g. Die _Schulkinder heute müssen hart arbeiten._

h. Tom ist _gerade heimgekommen_.

i. Er war _höchst zufrieden mit dem Ergebnis_ der Prüfung.

j. Andrew hatte fast einen Unfall, _als er im Ausland war._

k. Die _Freiheitsstatue_ ist sehr hoch.

l. Er _fährt täglich mit dem Zug_ zur Arbeit.

m. Die Kinder liefen _geradewegs über die Straße._

n. _Wenn ich nur mehr Zeit hätte!_

o. Maria scheint es _in letzter Zeit_ nicht sehr gut zu gehen.

126. WHERE DOES IT GO? An welche Stelle kommen die Adverbien?

a. I had time to put on my hat.
b. He last wrote to me in 1973 — that was a long time.
c. The attempt failed.
d. I could believe that it was happening to me.
e. Only fifty people entered the contest.
f. Some unhappy customers complained about the store's service.
g. When you make your choice, please choose.
h. He mentioned his stepfather.
i. Ryan is an impatient person and he's impolite.
j. We didn't have time to do much sightseeing.
k. He complained when he got bad service.
l. I hope to see you!
m. That was no accident - he did it.
n. I've only been there.
o. I realized what I've been doing wrong.

scarcely
ago
completely
hardly
surprisingly
rather
wisely
seldom
too
unfortunately
never
soon
deliberately
twice
yesterday

Lösung 127: a. would punch b. were c. were shining d. could/would hear e. would not be
f. were/was not g. could h. were/was i. would not be j. were not k. could l. would not have
m. would stop; could get n. would study; would be o. were

Lösung 126: a. I scarcely had ... b. ... a long time ago c. .. failed completely d. I could hardly believe ... e. Surprisingly, only ... f. Some rather unhappy customers ... g. ..., please choose wisely h. He seldom mentioned ... i. ... impolite, too j. Unfortunately, we ... k. He never complained ... l.... see you soon m. ... did it deliberately n. ... been there twice o. Yesterday, I realized ...

127. IF I WERE YOU Setzen Sie die Verben in der passenden Form ein!

a.	If I could box I _ _ _ _ _ him myself.	**punch**
b.	If I _ _ _ _ _ ill would you visit me?	**be**
c.	If the sun _ _ _ _ _ would you be happy?	**shine**
d.	If the door were open we _ _ _ _ _ them arguing.	**hear**
e.	If the window were shut it _ _ _ _ _ so cold in here.	**not be**
f.	I would travel home more often if flights _ _ _ _ _ so expensive.	**not be**
g.	If I had a book I _ _ _ _ _ read.	**can**
h.	It would be fun to watch TV if there _ _ _ _ _ something decent on.	**be**
i.	If you wore your good clothes less often I _ _ _ _ _ ironing all the time.	**not be**
j.	If motorbikes _ _ _ _ _ so loud I would buy one.	**not be**
k.	If the weather were nicer I think I _ _ _ _ _ live here.	**can**
l.	If there was enough milk in the bottle we _ _ _ _ _ to go shopping.	**not have**
m.	If you _ _ _ _ _ talking maybe I _ _ _ _ _ a word in.	**stop; get**
n.	If Dave _ _ _ _ _ harder his grades _ _ _ _ _ better.	**study; be**
o.	I'd try it if there _ _ _ _ _ any chance it would work.	**be**

128. SETZEN SIE DAS ADVERB EIN Wir geben Ihnen bei der Wortwahl eine kleine Hilfe!

a. I arrived l _ _ for my meeting. It was almost over.
b. We ba_ _ _ managed to catch the train in time.
c. Walter is se_ _ _ worried about his future.
d. She is breathing irreg_ _ _ and the doctor is worried.
e. Drive f_ _ _, or the police will catch us!
f. My Uncle Tim was b_ _ _ injured in a car crash last week.
g. The newspapers arrive fa_ _ _ quickly when you think how far it is to London.
h. This is a tr_ _ _ amazing book!
i. Tom is cer_ _ _ capable of completing the task.
j. Rosaline was hi_ _ _ surprised to see me.
k. He will d_ _ _ distribute the foodstuffs once they arrive.
l. They marched down the road, br_ _ _ heading for the bank.
m. Profits have decreased con_ _ _ this year.
n. This is a wh_ _ _ unsatisfactory case.
o. The children sp_ _ _ cleared away their toys.

Lösung 129: a. may b. may not/must not c. are you allowed to d. will be allowed to
e. Would John be allowed to f. may/can g. had been allowed to h. may I not i. might/may
j. was allowed to k. may l. are not allowed to m. may not n. am not allowed to o. are allowed to

Lösung 128: a. late b. barely c. seriously d. irregularly e. fast f. badly g. fairly h. truly i. certainly
j. highly k. duly l. briskly m. considerably n. wholly o. speedily

129. MAY, MIGHT, BE ALLOWED TO Bilden Sie Sätze mit diesen Formen!

a. _ _ _ _ _ _ we borrow your torch?   **Dürfen**

b. Children _ _ _ _ _ _ ride the carousel without a parent being present.   **dürfen nicht**

c. _ _ _ _ _ _ you watch horror movies?   **Dürft**

d. Perhaps we _ _ _ _ _ _ do it when we are older.   **werden dürfen**

e. _ _ _ _ _ _ John smoke cigarettes at home?   **Dürfte**

f. _ _ _ _ _ _ Kevin park here?   **Darf**

g. If I _ _ _ _ _ _ I would have spent a year in America.   **gedurft hätte**

h. Why _ _ _ _ _ _ I drive the car tonight?   **darf nicht**

i. You should listen to your teacher. You _ _ _ _ _ _ learn something.   **vielleicht**

j. When Catherine was a small girl she _ _ _ _ _ _ ride horses.   **durfte**

k. You _ _ _ _ _ _ go - I want to be alone.   **darfst**

l. In basketball you _ _ _ _ _ _ run with the ball.   **darfst nicht**

m. You _ _ _ _ _ _ stop working until I give permission!   **darfst nicht**

n. I _ _ _ _ _ _ comment on the matter.   **darf nicht**

o. Tom's poodles _ _ _ _ _ _ sit on the couch.   **dürfen**

a. It took Mark two weeks to get _ _ _ _ _ his illness.

b. I could really go _ _ _ _ _ a hot cup of coffee.

c. The police decided they would look _ _ _ _ _ the matter.

d. I ran _ _ _ _ _ Sarah in town.

e. She said she would see _ _ _ _ _ that her husband got the letter.

f. Jeff takes _ _ _ _ _ his mother. They look exactly alike.

g. The red car was catching _ _ _ _ _ the leader.

h. I would like to ring _ _ _ _ _ my boyfriend.

i. But he always gives _ _ _ _ _ his mother who says "Girls shouldn't ring boys!"

j. She drew _ _ _ _ _ when she saw the knife in his hand.

k. Only seven of his friends turned _ _ _ _ _ for his birthday party.

l. My sister and my brother never get _ _ _ _ _ each other.

m. The little boy couldn't keep _ _ _ _ _ the older ones in the race.

n. These exercises take _ _ _ _ _ an awful lot of time!

o. Hercules had to clean _ _ _ _ _ the Augean stables.

Lösung 131: a. done b. have you been c. have been d. Have you ever travelled e. has passed f. have you known g. has played h. Have you ever seen i. has worked j. Have you written k. have you cut l. has just won m. have taken n. Have you had o. has brought

131. PRESENT PERFECT Setzen Sie die Verben ins Present Perfect!

a. Have you _ _ _ _ _ _ the dishes? — *do*

b. Your clothes are filthy! Where _ _ _ _ _ _? — *be*

c. I _ _ _ _ _ _ to London to see the Queen. — *be*

d. You ever _ _ _ _ _ _ to Bombay? — *travel*

e. Susan _ _ _ _ _ _ her exams. — *pass*

f. How long you _ _ _ _ _ _ your current boyfriend? — *know*

g. He _ _ _ _ _ _ the three of hearts. — *play*

h. You ever _ _ _ _ _ _ real gold? — *see*

i. My brother Tony _ _ _ _ _ _ for the same firm all his life. — *work*

j. You _ _ _ _ _ _ to Cathy yet? — *write*

k. How often you _ _ _ _ _ _ the grass this summer? — *cut*

l. Tim just _ _ _ _ _ _ the election. — *win*

m. Kelly and Chad _ _ _ _ _ _ their son to the doctor. — *take*

n. You _ _ _ _ _ _ enough to drink? — *have*

o. Claudia _ _ _ _ _ _ the cat in. — *bring*

132. FLY, FLEW, FLOWN Wie lauten die Stammformen?

a. build, _____ _____
b. creep, crept, _____
c. drive, _____ driven
d. fling, _____ flung
e. go, _____ gone
f. grow, _____ grown
g. keep, kept, _____
h. _____ lay, lain

i. run, _____ run
j. say, said, _____
k. speed, sped
l. _____ stole, stolen
m. swear, swore, _____
n. tell, _____ told
o. weep, wept, _____

Lösung 133: a. is drunk b. is spoken c. will be opened d. was sent e. was met f. is being shown
g. was given h. is taught i. was interviewed j. is treated k. be exhibited l. was disproven
m. was written n. was made o. was designed

133. THE PASSIVE VOICE Vervollständigen Sie folgende Passivsätze!

a. In Germany, beer _ _ _ _ _ _ by many people. — **drink**

b. French _ _ _ _ _ _ in France. — **speak**

c. The Embassy _ _ _ _ _ _ next week. — **open**

d. A letter _ _ _ _ _ _ to my address. — **send**

e. The ambassador _ _ _ _ _ _ at the airport yesterday. — **meet**

f. The exhibit _ _ _ _ _ _ at the museum at the moment. — **show**

g. The child _ _ _ _ _ _ an ice-cream yesterday by an old man. — **give**

h. English _ _ _ _ _ _ all over the world. — **teach**

i. Yesterday, I _ _ _ _ _ _ by the local newspaper. — **interview**

j. Our dog _ _ _ _ _ _ very well by us. — **treat**

k. Many van Gogh paintings will _ _ _ _ _ _ in this gallery next year. — **exhibit**

l. Dr. Cogley's theory _ _ _ _ _ _ some years later. — **disprove**

m. "The Sign of Four" _ _ _ _ _ _ by Arthur Conan Doyle. — **write**

n. The decision _ _ _ _ _ _ by a well-respected committee. — **make**

o. The Lamborghini _ _ _ _ _ _ by Italians. — **design**

134. IRREGULAR VERBS Wie heißen die Stammformen dieser Verben?

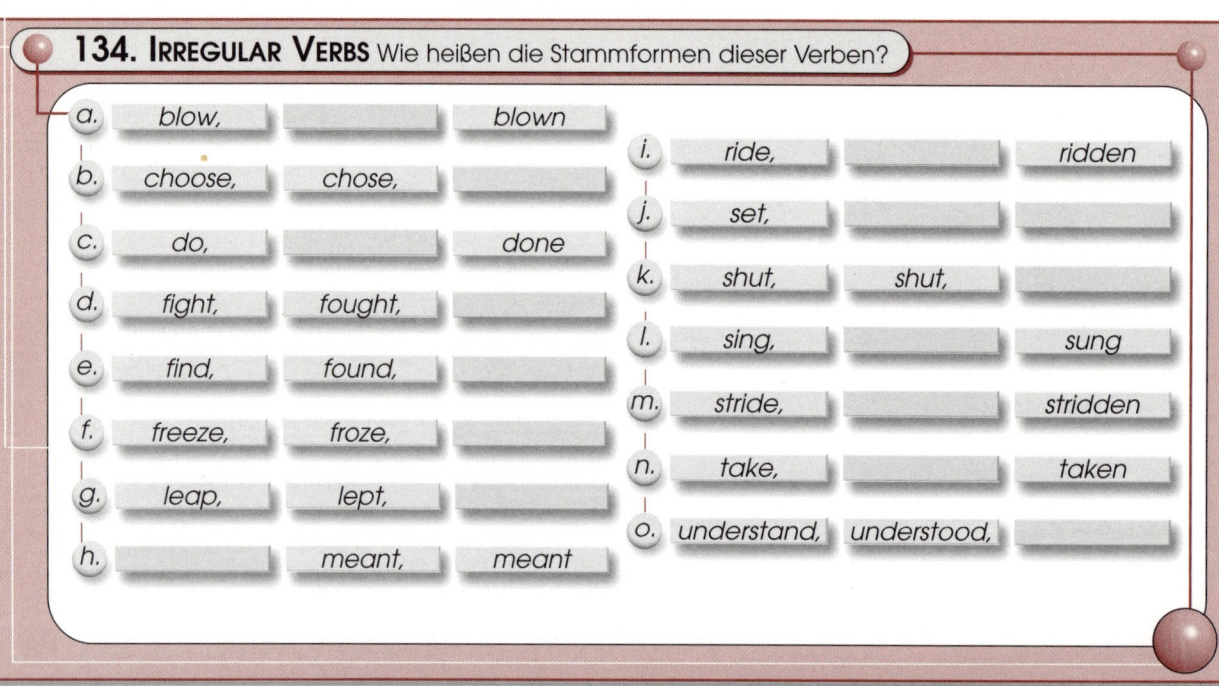

a. blow, _____, blown

b. choose, chose, _____

c. do, _____, done

d. fight, fought, _____

e. find, found, _____

f. freeze, froze, _____

g. leap, lept, _____

h. _____, meant, meant

i. ride, _____, ridden

j. set, _____, _____

k. shut, shut, _____

l. sing, _____, sung

m. stride, _____, stridden

n. take, _____, taken

o. understand, understood, _____

Lösung 135: a. has been doing b. have been ringing c. has been touring d. has been looking e. has been biting f. have you been going g. has been singing h. Has Richard been fighting i. has been working j. Have you been speaking k. Has Abe been cutting l. have been speaking m. have been swimming n. Have you been drinking o. has been crying

Lösung 134: a. blew b. chosen c. did d. fought e. found f. frozen g. leapt h. mean i. rode j. set, set k. shut l. sang m. strode n. took o. understood

135. PRESENT PERFECT CONTINUOUS Wie heißen die Verben im Present Perfect Continuous?

a. Who _ _ _ _ _ _ _ _ the dishes while I was away? — do

b. I _ _ _ _ _ _ _ _ all afternoon and can get no reply. — ring

c. Ken _ _ _ _ _ _ _ _ London all day and is exhausted. — tour

d. Richard _ _ _ _ _ _ _ _ for you everywhere. — look

e. Susan _ _ _ _ _ _ _ _ her nails all morning waiting for results. — bite

f. How long _ _ _ _ _ _ _ _ out with your current boyfriend? — go

g. He _ _ _ _ _ _ _ _ that song all day. — sing

h. Richard _ _ _ _ _ _ _ _? He's covered in scratches. — fighting

i. My brother Tony _ _ _ _ _ _ _ _ for the same firm all his life. — work

j. You _ _ _ _ _ _ _ _ to Jessica? — speak

k. Abe _ _ _ _ _ _ _ _ the grass? His shoes are all green. — cut

l. We _ _ _ _ _ _ _ _ with Kevin. — speak

m. Kelly and Chad _ _ _ _ _ _ _ _ with their son. — swim

n. You _ _ _ _ _ _ _ _? You reek of beer. — drink

o. Claudia _ _ _ _ _ _ _ _. Why? — cry

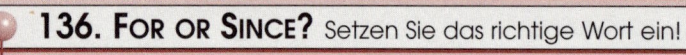

a. We've been working at this project _ _ _ _ last May.
b. I've been attending university _ _ _ _ over two years.
c. The game has been stopped _ _ _ _ twenty minutes due to snow.
d. The protest has been in progress _ _ _ _ two hours now.
e. I've been smoking _ _ _ _ years, _ _ _ _ I was fifteen in fact.
f. The post has been late every day _ _ _ _ the past week.
g. The present queen has reigned _ _ _ _ 1953.
h. Man has fought wars _ _ _ _ as long as anyone can remember.
i. She has been living here _ _ _ _ April.
j. I have been writing books _ _ _ _ 1998.
k. That castle has been there _ _ _ _ over six hundred years.
l. Schools have changed _ _ _ _ I was a schoolboy.
m. The television has been out of order _ _ _ _ weeks.
n. I have been waiting here _ _ _ _ 2.30.
o. He has worked like a beaver _ _ _ _ lunchtime.

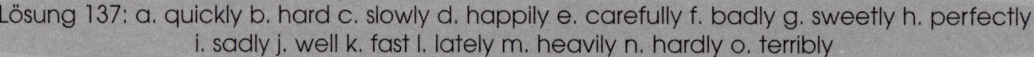

137. SETZEN SIE DAS ADVERB EIN. Der erste Buchstabe soll bei der Wortwahl helfen!

a. I worked q_ _ _ _ and was finished first.
b. John trains h_ _ _ _ before each race.
c. He speaks sl_ _ _ _ when speaking German.
d. Terry smiled h_ _ _ _ the day of his wedding.
e. Justin has been driving c_ _ _ _ since the crash.
f. He did b_ _ _ _ on the test and failed.
g. The birds are singing sw_ _ _ _ this morning.
h. Susan dances pe_ _ _ _. She doesn't make any mistakes.
i. Terry spoke s_ _ _ _ to Helen about the day of their divorce.
j. Matt speaks English very w_ _ _ _ .
k. One can travel f_ _ _ _ on a motorbike.
l. Have you written to Eileen l_ _ _ _? In the past few weeks I mean.
m. It snowed he_ _ _ _ on Christmas Day.
n. I ha_ _ _ _ recognized Carmen the last time I saw her.
o. She looked te_ _ _ _ ill.

138. HEARSAY Bilden Sie die indirekte Rede der folgenden Sätze!

a. The house was built in 1962.
b. It has a big garden.
c. It will be sold soon.
d. The match began on time.
e. Swiss radio broadcasts the programme.
f. The thief hit me.
g. Snow is falling outside at the moment.
h. Last year I went to visit my uncle.
i. Before the show started Tim left.
j. The coffee will be ready in a minute.
k. A storm caused the pylon to fall.
l. You must take a look at it.
m. The company gave us a hard time.
n. Petrol will rise in price tomorrow.
o. The wedding was very nice.

a. Tom told me that the house _____
b. He knew that it _____
c. He thought that it _____
d. I heard that the match _____
e. I told you that Swiss radio _____
f. She said that the thief _____
g. John said that snow _____
h. Bob said that he _____
i. He said that before the show _____
j. Mary told me that the coffee _____
k. I claimed that a storm _____
l. He said that I _____
m. We told you that the company _____
n. The newsreader said that patrol _____
o. She said that the wedding _____

Lösung 139: a. awoken b. beaten c. bled d. caught; caught e. dug f. felt g. forgave h. hear
i. led; led j. made k. sent l. shrunk m. slung n. split o. wrote

139. Welche Stammformen haben diese Verben?

a. awake, awoke, _____

b. beat, beat, _____

c. bleed, bled, _____

d. catch, _____, _____

e. dig, dug, _____

f. feel, _____, felt

g. forgive, _____, forgiven

h. _____, heard, heard

i. lead, _____, _____

j. make, made, _____

k. send, _____, sent

l. shrink, shrank, _____

m. sling, _____, slung,

n. split, split, _____

o. write, _____, written

140. IN OTHER WORDS Welche Aussage ist synonym?

a, I found it easily.

1. I simply found it.
2. I found it easy.
3. I found it with ease.

b, I'd better do it myself.

1. In my opinion I'd better do it.
2. I'd better do it personally.
3. If I did it, I'd do it better.

c, Tomorrow or today? The latter!

1. Today!
2. The later of the two!
3. Neither!

d, He asked me, oddly enough.

1. He asked me in an odd manner.
2. He asked me, which is odd.
3. He asked how odd it was.

e, He'd been gone for some time.

1. He would have left a while ago.
2. He hadn't been here in a while.
3. He went - I'm not sure how long.

f, It is known to be true.

1. Truthfulness makes one well-known.
2. It knows what's true and what isn't.
3. Everyone knows that that's correct.

Lösung 140 a. 3 b. 2 c. 1 d. 2 e. 2 f. 3